Helping Christians Grow

CHRISTIAN EDUCATION

AN INDEPENDENT-STUDY TEXTBOOK

by Dwayne E. Turner

---

*Developed in Cooperation With
the ICI International Office Staff*

*Instructional Development Specialist:
David D. Duncan*

Illustrator: Rick Allen

International Correspondence Institute
Chaussée de Waterloo, 45
1640 Rhode-Saint-Genèse
(Brussels) Belgium

First Edition 1984
  Reprinted 1985
  Reprinted 1991

S0034E90   ISBN 1-56390-033-5

Table of Contents

THE ICI CHRISTIAN SERVICE PROGRAM

 This is one of 18 courses (subjects) that make up the ICI Christian Service Program. The symbol at the left is a guide for order of study in the series, which is divided into three units of six courses each. *Helping Christians Grow: Christian Education* is Course 4 in Unit III. You will benefit by studying the courses in their proper order.

Study materials in the Christian Service Program have been prepared in a self-teaching format especially for Christian workers. These courses provide a student with Bible knowledge and skills needed for practical Christian service. You may study this course in order to receive credit toward a certificate, or for personal enrichment.

ATTENTION

Please read the course introduction very carefully. It is important that you follow these instructions so you can achieve the goals of the course, and be prepared for the student unit reports.

Address all correspondence concerning the course to your ICI instructor at the address stamped below. In case it is not shown, and you do not have the address of the ICI office in your area, then please write to the following address:

International Correspondence Institute
Chaussée de Waterloo, 45
1640 Rhode-Saint-Genèse
(Brussels) Belgium

The address of your local ICI office is:

Course Introduction

Have you wondered, "Why does the church include teaching programs in its ministry?" or "How does teaching relate to what the church is seeking to accomplish?" Christian nurturing is very important to the church's ministry. The teaching ministry helps us grow and mature in the Christian faith. It is also very helpful in preparing and training us to become involved in outreach ministries to other people. Studying this course will help you to grow toward spiritual maturity and to become aware of your own need for more Christian teaching. It will also help train and equip you to take advantage of opportunities to involve yourself in teaching others about the Christian faith.

Christians recognize the Bible as the highest authority in matters of the Christian faith and practice. They try to build ministries on concepts and principles from the Bible. In this course you will gain a better understanding of the Christian nurturing ministry by studying directly from the Bible and by studying some practical matters about teaching and learning.

Teaching methods where you live may not be the same as those with which I am familiar. However, the Bible gives us broad principles to direct our ministries. As a result, we have plenty of room to apply those principles in different methods as need requires. As we examine the nature of spiritual life and principles of Christian growth, we shall evaluate some biblical guidelines for the development and growth of our spiritual life. In addition, we shall consider biblical principles for nurturing Christian growth in others and ways to apply those principles right where we are to meet people's spiritual needs.

Course Description

Helping Christians Grow: Christian Education is a study of the biblical basis for the nurturing ministry and the practical application of teaching in the church today. It gives emphasis to the needs of the pupils in various stages of human development and to the various opportunities for Christian nurturing through the ministry of local church programs, sharing groups, and the Christian home.

Course Objectives

When you finish this course you should be able to:

1. Understand the biblical rationale for Christian nurture.

2. Explain how Christian nurture relates to teaching-learning theory and processes.

3. Recognize and take advantage of opportunities available to you to nurture the spiritual life of others.

4. Relate nurturing to the growth and development process of natural and spiritual life.

5. Know the importance and effects of Christian nurture in the interaction between the teacher and the learner.

6. Discuss the role of Christian nurture as it applies to family relationships.

Textbooks

You will use *Helping Christians Grow: Christian Education* by Dwayne E. Turner as both the textbook and study guide for this course. The Bible is the only other textbook required. Scriptures quoted are from the *New International Version*, 1978 edition, unless otherwise noted.

Study Time

How much time you actually need to study each lesson depends in part on your knowledge of the subject and the strength of your study skills before you begin this course. The time you spend also depends on the extent to which you follow directions and develop skills necessary for independent study. Plan your study schedule so that you spend enough time to reach the objectives stated by the author of the course and your personal objectives as well.

Lesson Organization and Study Pattern

Each lesson includes: 1) lesson title, 2) opening statement, 3) lesson outline, 4) lesson objectives, 5) learning activities, 6) key words, 7) lesson development including study questions, 8) self-test (at the end of the lesson development), and 9) answers to the study questions.

The lesson outline and objectives will give you an overview of the subject, help you to focus your attention on the most important points as you study, and tell you what you should learn.

Most of the study questions in the lesson development can be answered in spaces provided in this study guide. Longer answers should be written in a notebook. As you write the answers in your notebook, be sure to record the number and title of the lesson. This will help you in your review for the unit student report.

Do not look ahead at the answers until you have given your answer. If you give your own answers, you will remember what you study much better. After you have answered the study questions, check your answers with those given at the end of the lesson. Then correct those you did not answer correctly. The answers are not given in the usual numerical order, so that you will not accidentally see the answer to the next question.

These study questions are very important. They will help you to remember the main ideas presented in the lesson, and to apply the principles you have learned.

How to Answer Questions

There are different kinds of study questions and self-test questions in this study guide. Below are samples of several types and how to answer them. Specific instructions will be given for other types of questions that may occur.

A *MULTIPLE CHOICE* question or item asks you to choose an answer from the ones that are given.

Example

1 A week has a total of
a) 10 days.
b) 7 days.
c) 5 days.

The correct answer is *b) 7 days.* In your study guide, make a circle around *b)* as shown here:

1 A week has a total of
a) 10 days.
(b)) 7 days.
c) 5 days.

(For some multiple-choice items, more than one answer will be correct. In that case, you would circle the letter in front of each correct answer.)

A *TRUE-FALSE* question or item asks you to choose which of several statements are TRUE.

Example

2 Which statements below are TRUE?
a The Bible has a total of 120 books.
(**b**) The Bible is a message for believers today.
c All of the Bible authors wrote in the Hebrew language.
(**d**) The Holy Spirit inspired the writers of the Bible.

Statements **b** and **d** are true. You would make a circle around these two letters to show your choices, as you see above.

A *MATCHING* question or item asks you to match things that go together, such as names with descriptions, or Bible books with their authors.

Example

3 Write the number for the leader's name in front of each phrase that describes something he did.

..*1*..**a** Received the Law at Mt. Sinai   1) Moses

..*2*..**b** Led the Israelites across Jordan   2) Joshua

..*2*..**c** Marched around Jericho

..*1*..**d** Lived in Pharaoh's court

Phrases **a** and **d** refer to Moses, and phrases **b** and **c** refer to Joshua. You would write **1** beside **a** and **d**, and **2** beside **b** and **c**, as you see above.

Ways to study this course

If you study this ICI course by yourself, all of your work can be completed by mail. Although ICI has designed this course for you to study on your own, you may also study it in a group or class. If you do this, the instructor may give you added instructions besides those in the course. If so, be sure to follow his instructions.

Possibly you are interested in using the course in a home Bible study group, in a class at church, or in a Bible school. You will find both the subject content and study methods excellent for these purposes.

Unit Student Reports

If you are studying independently with ICI, with a group, or in a class, you have received with this course your unit student reports. These are to be answered according to the directions included in the course and in the unit student reports. You should complete and send your answer sheets to your instructor for his correction and suggestions regarding your work.

Certificate

Upon the successful completion of the course and the final grading of the unit student report by your ICI instructor, you will receive your Certificate of Award.

Author of This Course

Dwayne E. Turner writes from a broad background of training and experience in the field of Christian education. He has served churches as pastor, associate pastor, and minister of Christian education, gaining experience in various facets of the ministry. He was ordained in 1970.

From 1968 to 1974 Mr. Turner served on the faculty of Northwest College, Kirkland, Washington. In 1975 he commenced his missionary career as he moved to Cebu City, Republic of the Philippines, where he served for three years as the Administrative Dean of Immanuel Bible College. As a missionary educator, Mr. Turner has been involved with curriculum development for Christian education in the Philippines.

Mr. Turner earned a bachelor of arts degree in Bible and Theology from North Central Bible College in Minneapolis, Minnesota and his M.R.E. degree from Conservative Baptist Theological Seminary in Denver, Colorado. He has an M.A. degree in missions from the Assemblies of God Graduate School in Springfield, Missouri, and is presently a candidate for a doctor of ministry degree at Conservative Baptist Theological Seminary. He is married and has two sons.

Your ICI Instructor

Your ICI instructor will be happy to help you in any way possible. If you have any questions about the course or the unit student reports, please feel free to ask him. If several people want to study this course together, ask about special arrangements for group study.

God bless you as you begin to study *Helping Christians Grow: Christian Education*. May it enrich your life and Christian service and help you to fulfill more effectively your part in the body of Christ.

Unit 1

NURTURING SPIRITUAL GROWTH

LESSON 1

Alive and Growing

Juan and Maria were enthralled with their new baby son. His birth was a happy event in their home. Words could hardly describe the thrill of new life they shared. Yet they were very aware of the responsibilities that rested on them. The infant's survival depended on them: on the care they gave and on the provisions they made for his needs.

How quickly he grew! Maria could almost see him develop. Day by day he gained weight and grew larger, developing in the healthful environment under the influence of loving care.

We might expect that as the weeks extended into months and years, normal growth and development would occur. It would not be too difficult to look at Juan and imagine how the boy might appear after several years. The baby was alive and growing!

In a similar way, the normal expectation of spiritual life is growth toward spiritual maturity. In this lesson you will discover that new spiritual life must be nurtured for growth to occur, and you will learn what is needed to nurture spiritual growth.

lesson outline

The Nature of Spiritual Growth
Nurture and Spiritual Growth
Elements of Spiritual Growth

lesson objectives

When you finish this lesson you should be able to:

- Identify statements which explain the nature of and the need for spiritual growth.

- Explain the significance of the ministry of nurturing spiritual life.

- Recognize the characteristics of the various levels of spiritual growth.

- Identify the elements of spiritual growth and relate one's spiritual progress to the role of these elements.

15

learning activities

1. Carefully read the preliminary section in this independent-study textbook. You will find examples of the kinds of study questions used in this textbook and how to answer each one.

2. Read carefully the opening pages of this lesson and the outline which is given. Read also the objectives, both the lesson objectives which are listed at the beginning of the lesson and the enabling objectives which are given through the lesson. These objectives tell you what you should be able to do after you have studied the lesson. The study questions and the self-test are based on them.

3. Some key words are listed at the beginning of the lesson. You will find their definitions in the glossary at the end of this study guide. Be sure to find the meanings of any words that are not familiar to you.

4. Read the lesson and do the exercises in the lesson development. Be sure to read Bible portions as you are instructed. This is necessary to gain a full understanding of the lesson material. Write answers to questions in this study where space is provided. Write longer answers in a notebook. You will get more out of the course if you make it a practice to put something of your own into writing before you look ahead to the answers. Check your answers with those given at the end of the lesson.

5. Take the self-test at the end of the lesson. Check your answers carefully with those provided at the back of this study guide.

key words

admonished	disclosure	nutritious
adversity	discriminate	paradoxically
bereaved	durability	potential
boredom	emaciated	prolonged
characteristics	enthralled	propositions
compatible	explicitly	reservoir

16

contentious	facilitate	stature
corporate	inherent	survive
counterpart	latent	transition
degeneration	nurture	vitality

lesson development

THE NATURE OF SPIRITUAL GROWTH

The Standard for Spiritual Growth

Objective 1. *Identify statements which give the biblical standard for spiritual life and those which describe how the new Christian can experience the quality of life his Lord intends for him.*

When you heard and believed the Christian good news, you began living an exciting new life. This experience is called *new birth* or *spiritual birth*. Everyone who shares this new life in Christ begins by being born spiritually. Unlike biological life, which is limited by time to a normal life cycle, the germ of spiritual life is eternal. In people this germ of spiritual life resembles human infancy: it is subject to growth, development, and maturity.

Jesus spoke specifically to the possibilities inherent in this germ of life: "I have come that they may have life, and have it to the full" (John 10:10). You brought to Him a life filled with sin that had separated you from Him. He has given you a new life, His life, and He wants you to have this abundant new life to the fullest.

When we speak of *life to the fullest*, we refer to the quality of life one can experience. Physical life, as we all know, can be sustained at a bare existence level for some time. However, at this level one couldn't be very active, produce significantly, or truly enjoy life. This is life at a very low level. By contrast, when one eats well, lives in a healthful, secure environment, and exercises properly, he develops an abundant reservoir of energy. He feels great. He is active, energetic, and able to address his tasks heartily. He grows, develops, and matures according to normal expectations. He thrives! In this condition he fulfills the purpose for which he was designed. He is experiencing *life to the fullest*.

When you were born spiritually, the spirit of Jesus Christ came to live in you. This birth generated the potential for spiritual development—development into the likeness of Jesus Christ (Colossians 1:27). Now that the spirit of Jesus resides in you, He assumes control of your life. As the Lord of your life, He lives His life out through you as far as you surrender to His Lordship over your life (Romans 8:9-11).

Think for a moment of a newborn infant. Who can tell what the future may hold for that child? He is a bundle of potential and capabilities which need development. Given proper care and nourishment, a healthful environment, adequate encouragement, and ample opportunities, the child will develop into a whole, mature person. This baby has within him everything he will ever become, but in latent form which must be developed.

We can transfer the idea of a newborn infant's growth and development toward maturity to spiritual life. Our Lord wants each of us to experience life to the fullest. How does one experience fullness of spiritual life? As we have noted above you began to live the new life when you experienced new birth. You began like a spiritual baby, as a babe in Christ. In every way you were completely God's child. Yet you were not fully developed. To experience the fullness of the new life, spiritual growth and development must occur.

In general, as one responds to the Spirit's control of his life, he begins to grow spiritually. Under the Spirit's control, he is in a favorable environment; nevertheless, he needs spiritual nourishment. As he grows he becomes aware not only of his marvelous privileges but also of his responsibilities. His understanding of spiritual life expands as his knowledge of God's Word increases. God's purpose for his life becomes increasingly clearer as he walks with the Spirit in control of his life (Galatians 5:25). The germ of spiritual life, like its physical counterpart, must be nourished, nurtured, and exercised for optimum development that leads to productive maturity, as we shall see.

1 Circle the letter in front of each TRUE statement.

a From Scripture we learn that spiritual life comes to each person fully developed and complete, leaving no room for improvement.

b Jesus indicated that there are no levels of spiritual life; therefore, when one is born again, he experiences life to the fullest automatically and immediately.

c From Scripture we learn that our Lord has made provision for us to experience a rich and full spiritual life, but this potential is subject to growth, development, and maturity.

d As one invites the Spirit of Jesus to assume and maintain control of his life, he is in a position to develop spiritually.

e The newly born Christian develops and matures spiritually as he is spiritually nourished and nurtured in an environment which encourages spiritual growth and as he responds positively to the desires of the Spirit as He leads them into deeper spiritual experiences.

The Need for Spiritual Growth

Objective 2. *Recognize the correct explanation of the need for spiritual growth as it is outlined in this text.*

Can you imagine a baby who does not grow? Can you think of a person who is several years old but has not developed beyond the infancy stage? Immediately you would recognize that something was wrong. You would respond in this way because we expect growth and development to accompany life. That which is alive and normal will grow and progress toward maturity.

Jesus taught the principle of spiritual growth to His disciples. He compared spiritual life to a vine and its branches, saying that no individual branch on the vine can be productive in and of itself.

It must be in vital contact with the life of the vine. Then it can produce ever more abundantly as it develops and matures. In the same way, no Christian can mature and be spiritually productive apart from *remaining in vital contact with the true Vine, Jesus Christ* (John 15:1-16, but notice especially vs. 4, 5, 8, and 16). The only alternative to spiritual growth and development is spiritual decay, degeneration, and finally spiritual death (John 15:2, 6).

We understand that a person is not an infant one day and an adult the next. Development toward maturity involves a time-consuming process of growth. Spiritual life develops according to this same growth principle. While we begin as babes, growth and development are to be expected. Just as a baby grows toward adulthood, so a babe in Christ must grow toward spiritual maturity. We expect this growth because the person is spiritually alive. And what is alive and normal grows, develops, and matures as long as it is nourished properly and nurtured in the Spirit-controlled environment. Then, and only then, can one accomplish the spiritual purpose for which God has called him. He is thus able to bear lasting fruit such as the Father desires (John 15:16), and God's work on earth can be accomplished.

2-3 Circle the letter of the correct answer for each question.

2 We normally expect what is alive will
a) remain in a stage of infancy.
b) grow and develop toward maturity.
c) be brought immediately to maturity.
d) produce little if any observable change.

3 Spiritual growth is needed since it is commanded by the Lord Jesus and because it (choose the best answer)
a) is an almost automatic process that is initiated by the new birth experience.
b) is challenging to fully develop one's spiritual potential and to enjoy the benefits of spiritual vitality that accompany such development.
c) enables one to accomplish successfully the Lord's purpose for his life and to do the Lord's work effectively.

NURTURE AND SPIRITUAL GROWTH

Objective 3. *Select statements which explain correctly why spiritual life must be nurtured.*

Every mother knows that if her baby is to survive and grow, his new life must be nurtured. A newborn baby is helpless and must depend on others to supply his survival needs. Because of this, mothers lovingly care for their babies by supplying food and by providing for their total needs. Without such tender care babies would soon die. Newborn babes are helpless and require nurture!

In a similar way, spiritual life needs nurture. Helping someone experience spiritual birth is but the beginning of our Christian responsibility to the person. Following new birth comes the need to nurture spiritual life so the person will survive spiritually and grow toward Christian maturity. While spiritual infants are fully God's children, they have just begun to develop their spiritual potential and do not yet experience spiritual life to the full, as their Lord intends. During the early stages of development, they need the support of caring spiritual brothers and sisters, who lend spiritual support and encouragement. With this support and appropriate spiritual nourishment, they develop spiritual stature. Nurture of spiritual life is thus needed for new converts to survive spiritually and to grow and develop toward Christian maturity.

If new life is properly nurtured, growth and development toward maturity may be expected. Such growth is predictable whether we are considering farm crops, animals, children, or new converts. The ministry of nurturing produces favorable conditions under which new spiritual life can grow toward full maturity.

You will recall, perhaps, Jesus' words to Peter concerning his ministry. The task of nurturing spiritual life involves people at various stages of Christian maturity from infant *lambs* to mature *sheep* (see John 21:15-17). Obviously, Peter understood the need and accepted the challenge to care for the total flock, for he mentions both the spiritual infants (1 Peter 2:2) and the rest of the flock (1 Peter 5:1-4). Moreover, Peter appeals to other Christian workers

21

to nurture spiritual life in the same way, for he knew that it must be nurtured to survive and to reach its full potential.

4 Circle the letter in front of each TRUE statement.

a Spiritual life has little or no durability to withstand testing until it is fully mature.

b In its infancy, spiritual life is somewhat frail and needs the suppport and encouragement of the Christian brotherhood until it develops spiritual stature.

c Spiritual life is maintained and developed by the ministry of Christian nurture.

d In the process of nurturing spiritual life, we provide the conditions for spiritual growth and development, but we can't really predict whether any good response will follow our efforts.

ELEMENTS OF SPIRITUAL GROWTH

Objective **4.** *Identify those elements of spiritual growth which lead one toward spiritual maturity.*

We have discussed the importance of those things which help sustain life: food, favorable environment, support during infancy, exercise, and loving nurture. Spiritual life, similarly, grows and matures normally when it has the necessary growth elements. It thrives on the Word of God, is nurtured by healthy Christian relationships, is stimulated by use (that is, as one prays, exercises his spiritual gifts, and applies knowledge of the Word to his own life), and abounds as it shares its life with others. Actually, the growth, development, and maturity of spiritual life is the normal response one would expect. It is also the fulfillment of our Lord's specific commandments. Thus, when one matures spiritually he completes the intended life cycle: birth, growth, development, maturity, and reproduction. He fulfills the purpose for which he exists. Such a response brings glory to God and is the only appropriate response one can make for the benefits given: salvation and eternal life. Before we discuss the elements of spiritual growth

22

in detail to see how effective they are in producing spiritual development and maturity, let's examine the levels of spiritual growth.

Levels of Spiritual Growth

Objective 5. *Recognize the various levels of spiritual growth and the appropriate characteristics and description of each.*

We are aware that nutritious food is essential to proper growth. A baby begins to receive food very soon after birth. This is essential to his survival and growth. We also recognize that there are levels of development through which a person passes as he develops toward maturity. One of the marks of these levels of development is the ability to receive and digest different types of foods. Infants can handle only milk, and milk is all they need to facilitate proper growth. But soon the baby requires something more substantial: cereal, porridge, or finely chopped vegetables and fruit. Later the child requires a fully balanced diet, which should include meat. Two basic facts emerge from these observations: 1) food is essential to proper growth and development, and 2) food must be appropriate for the stage of development.

23

Again the illustration transfers beautifully to spiritual life. Spiritual life requires spiritual food to nurture spiritual growth. However, spiritual food, as we have seen, must be appropriate to the level of spiritual development.

The Bible, God's Word, is compared to spiritual food. It is like milk for spiritual infants, and it is like solid food for those who are more mature spiritually.

5 Read 1 Corinthians 3:1-2, 1 Peter 2:2, Hebrews 5:12-14, and Ephesians 4:11-16 and answer the following questions which relate to these Scripture references.
a What two kinds of spiritual food are described in these verses?
.... *MILK & Solid* ....

b According to these Scripture references, ...*MILK*.......

is intended for those who are infants in Christ, while ...*Meat*

.....................*Solid*........................... is for the mature.
c The stronger diet is for the mature, those who have learned to

.... , so that they will be

prepared for .... so that the body of

Christ will be built up, until we all reach ....

.... and become mature, attaining

unto ....

Now that we have discussed the need for matching the spiritual food with the appropriate level of spiritual development, let's examine three levels of human existence that are described in 1 Corinthians 2:10—3:3: 1) *the man without the Spirit*, 2) *the worldly man*, and 3) *the spiritual man*. In these verses the apostle Paul describes the characteristics of each level. From this description we can determine what is needed to produce the spiritual growth and development that lead to full maturity.

The man we shall consider first is referred to as *the man without the Spirit*. He has not been born spiritually; therefore, he is spiritually dead (2:14). He is at the lowest level of human existence. The man at the second level is described as *worldly* (3:3). He has experienced the new birth and is therefore alive spiritually; however, he has not developed beyond the stage of spiritual infancy. At the third level we see *the spiritual man* (2:12,13,15). In the process of development he has gained spiritual stature, and he is able to function in more adult-like ways.

These Scriptures indicate that the ability to receive and understand spiritual truth is a major difference among these types. In fact, the ability to understand God's Word demonstrates which level of spiritual maturity a person has attained, if any. As you would expect, *the man without the Spirit* cannot understand or appreciate spiritual food, for his interests lie in other directions. Paradoxically, *the worldly man* is a *spiritual baby*. He must be fed with spiritual milk only. He is able to understand only elementary spiritual truth. He is interested in feeling good and enjoying the blessings of the Lord. But his attention span is short when he is faced with the sobering responsibilities of spiritual adulthood. Thus, he feels no obligation to grow spiritually and develop his spiritual muscles. He can postpone that serious business until later, when he is ready to get serious. *The spiritual man,* being more fully committed to his Lord, is maturing in his relationship with God. He is fully satisfied with the deeper doctrinal truths, the meat or solid food of God's Word. Moreover, he shares this truth with others, encourages those less mature than he, and is able to teach and serve effectively within the body of Christ.

Paul's teaching on the levels of spirituality shows us that God's Word is the spiritual food which nurtures spiritual growth. One's response to the Word, then, determines whether he will progress spiritually toward a healthy and productive period of Christian maturity or remain a spiritual infant with the dangerous signs that accompany prolonged infancy.

6 Match the descriptions and characteristics (left) with the appropriate level of spirituality (right).

2..**a** Operates at the "feeling" level of spirituality, hasn't truly assumed his spiritual responsibilities

1..**b** Doesn't understand or respond to spiritual things

3..**c** Enjoys the deeper truths of God's Word, exercises good judgment, and shares truth with others

1..**d** Hasn't experienced the new birth

2..**e** Has experienced the new birth, but has remained a spiritual infant

3..**f** Experience is marked by progress from spiritual infancy to spiritual maturity

1) Man without the Spirit
2) The worldly man
3) The spiritual man

7 Evaluate each example, identify the level of spiritual growth involved, and explain why you chose as you did.

a A noted non-Christian politician of England attended a service in which the Word of God was preached with clarity, power, and logic, under the anointing of the Holy Spirit, according to reputable witnesses. When the service ended, his host asked, "What did you think of the service?" He responded, "To tell you the truth, I gave the speaker my whole attention, but I could not get what he was trying to say." Though intellectually brilliant,

he was unable to respond. He is typical of man ....

.... Why?

....

....

b Pastor James recently moved to a new church. Many people in his congregation, he notices, respond well to general evangelistic preaching. Preaching on the deeper life in the Spirit and spiritual responsibilities, such as the commitment to work and witness in the community, however, meets with little enthusiasm. He notices

26

that when he ministers the truth about complete commitment to Christ, being faithful to church, giving service to the community, taking responsibility for leadership (teaching a Bible class, organizing a Bible study cell group, etc.), and supporting the Lord's work on a regular basis, his people get restless and very quiet. People who respond in this way have the characteristics of the .... man. Why?

....

....

c Dan belongs to a Bible-centered church. He is involved in a workers' training course to improve his skills to communicate more effectively to his junior boys' class. He has adopted a personal spiritual development plan that includes consistent Bible reading, prayer, and regular church attendance. His Christian life has been difficult at times because of family opposition, professional obstacles, and illness. In spite of the difficulties, Dan's testimony and life are a consistent witness to the reality of God's grace that mellow one in spite of hardship. Dan is an example of the

.... man. Why?

....

....

Nurture Through the Word

Objective 6. *Select statements which explain correctly how the Bible nurtures spiritual growth.*

In our discussion on the levels of spiritual development, we noted that God's Word is the spiritual food which nurtures spiritual growth. One's spiritual development is directly related to his response to the Word of God. Let's examine more closely how the Bible nurtures spiritual growth.

While the physical universe speaks forcefully of our Creator, this revelation is general and incomplete. In the Scriptures, however, God reveals Himself more fully. Whereas the physical universe speaks of qualities such as power and wisdom, the Bible reveals His holiness, justice, truth, mercy, and love, to name a few more of His qualities. The Scriptures also reveal God's nature, plan, and will for man. In this disclosure God reveals Himself.

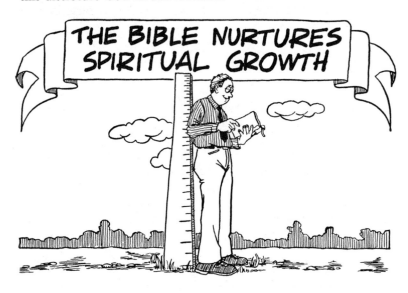

God's Word provides us with His plan for our lives. We learn how to serve Him acceptably, how to correct mistakes that hinder the development of our relationship with Him, the nature of spiritual life, what produces spiritual victory, and the goals of Christian living. In short, the Bible is God's blueprint for spiritual life.

The Scriptures nurture spiritual growth because they are quickened by God, and they are life-giving. The same spiritual life that resides in the Scriptures resides in the Christian. The life of God in the Word is the source of the new life God gives. The spiritual life within responds to the spiritual nourishment in the Word. It is a compatible diet; however, Christians must allow the Word to change what God intends. As they desire what God desires, they grow and develop in their likeness to Christ (2 Corinthians 3:18).

8 Circle the letter in front of each statement which explains how the Bible nurtures spiritual growth.

a) The Bible provides the nourishment required to sustain spiritual life and produce spiritual growth.

b) Biblical truth enables one to know God's will and respond to His purpose in an acceptable manner.

c) The life of God, inherent in His Word, corresponds to the life of God in each believer; therefore, as the believer allows the Word to change his life, he is able to be what God wants him to be.

d) The Bible affects spiritual growth by effecting a change in attitude in some believers as they assent to the rightness of its proposition about spiritual life.

Nurture Through Relationships

Objective 7. *Select statements which explain how relationships promote spiritual growth.*

When babies are born they are a part of a family. Each member makes room in his life to accept and accommodate this new family member. The family unit is the setting in which the needs of the newborn are met. Each member gives of himself to meet the needs of the new child and helps nurture his new life. Throughout the development of the child, the family provides the caring, supporting setting in which he can mature. The family experience is one of sharing mutual life, of nurturing one another, of meeting each other's needs. The strength of the family relationship is an important factor in nurturing new life.

With spiritual life, association with other Christians contributes to spiritual growth. The caring relationship mutually shared by fellow believers nurtures spiritual growth.

It is often helpful for a new Christian to identify closely with one who is spiritually more mature. In a sense, the more mature Christian can become like a spiritual parent, providing the loving, caring relationship which nurtures spiritual life. Such a person can aid the new Christian in studying and applying God's Word to his own situation, influence him by his godly example, and offer needed encouragement, counsel, and prayer.

29

God has planned, also, that the local church be a place where spiritual life is nurtured. Many Christians think of the church congregation as the family of God. So helping a new Christian identify with the local church can be compared to helping a new baby relate properly to his family. Local churches, as we have seen, are organized with God-appointed leaders, such as pastors, deacons, and teachers, to help Christians grow toward spiritual maturity (Ephesians 4:11-16). The activities of the church—study of the Word, corporate worship, active evangelism, effective service and education, fellowship, and discipline—are designed to accomplish one primary goal: nurture spiritual life and promote spiritual growth.

9 Circle the letter of each TRUE statement.

a One's spiritual growth is promoted by relationships because he is able to avoid difficult spiritual decisions, by permitting others to decide which is the right or wrong course of action.

b Spiritual life is nurtured by the associations one has with more mature Christians, who might be compared to good spiritual parents, giving advice, encouragement, love, and understanding.

c The church functions as a place where spiritual life is nurtured through study of the Word, corporate worship, effective service, and discipline.

d The church promotes growth by association. As one becomes a part of the church organization, he automatically grows in spiritual understanding and Christian maturity.

Nurture Through Use

Objective 8. *Distinguish between activities that help promote and those that do not promote spiritual growth.*

Perhaps you have been wondering: why have a healthy and potentially productive body? What is its function? Should it be used or should it be just a potential source of productivity? Should its purpose be to please itself only or does it have a responsibility to others? Will it's ability to function effectively be impaired if the body is not exercised? These and other questions come to mind as we consider spiritual life.

As we have seen, Jesus admonished His disciples to become productive. Not only is spiritual health involved in His admonition but also spiritual life (John 15:1-8). The point is that one must be fruitful or else he will suffer spiritual loss. Thus the goal of Christian growth and maturity is service and productivity. And just as Christians are admonished to grow and develop (2 Timothy 2:15; 2 Peter 3:18) so are they challenged to share the truth so that the world may know of God's redeeming grace (Matthew 28:19-20; Mark 16:15; Acts 1:8). While the writer to the Hebrews implies that mature Christians should be capable of and involved in teaching truth and exercising spiritual discernment (Hebrews 5:12), Paul says explicitly that the various church ministries exist "to prepare God's people for works of service, so that the body of Christ may be built up until we all reach unity in the faith and in the knowledge of the Son of God and become mature, attaining to the whole measure of the fullness of Christ" (Ephesians 4:12-13).

As Christians perceive their responsibilities to become Christ's ambassadors, they share the good news with others. Living, spiritual organisms that are healthy normally reproduce. They realize that the process of growth and maturity is not an end in itself. They live to exalt the Author of life and share His life constantly with those who have not experienced its life-changing power. The mature Christian thus fulfills the purpose for which he was born. Alive and growing, he moves purposefully to do his Lord's will: building up the body of Christ spiritually and numerically.

10 Circle the letter in front of each example of Christian activity that truly exercises spiritual life and promotes spiritual growth.

a) Bob attends church regularly and studies the Word of God consistently. He conducts a Bible study during the lunch hour at his job. He shares his salvation experience whenever he has the opportunity. He initiated a good devotional time daily for his family soon after he accepted Christ. His family is sensitive to the needs of others and continually seeks to help others.

b) Richard has been a Christian for many years. He makes an effort to attend church when he feels he can. He has never witnessed to others, nor has he become involved in Bible study, regular

31

devotions, or church activities (both fellowship and service). He doesn't feel that he should be obligated to support the ministries of the church, for he sees the relationship as one of "association" only. His friends view him as they would any other non-Christian, for there is little to distinguish him from them.

11 Spiritual growth is promoted by (circle the letters of the best completions)
a) simply increasing one's knowledge of spiritual life, purpose, destiny.
b) the knowledge that one is saved to serve and share with others and to apply the knowledge gained.
c) helping others, especially those who are spiritual infants, to grow and develop spiritually.
d) one's studies to increase his knowledge of the truth so that he will be an effective spiritual worker.

12 Identify the elements of spiritual growth we have studied in this section by placing a 1) in front of those activities that truly promote maturity and a 2) in front of those that do not lead to maturity.

.... **a** Campaigning as a candidate for a church office which promises to keep one in the public eye
.... **b** Studying the Word consistently and allowing it to become the standard for one's life and service
.... **c** Sharing the gospel with others who neither know its claims nor its power to change their lives
.... **d** Making efforts to keep busy doing such things as promoting church money-raising functions, organizing parties for members, initiating discussion groups which consider popular books and social action issues and the attempt to bridge the gap between the church and the world by nonspiritual means
.... **e** Nurturing spiritual life by teaching newborn spiritual babes the truths they need to know to survive spiritually and to grow toward life to the fullest
.... **f** Serving the body: helping the poor, the sick, the elderly, the bereaved, and the discouraged

self-test

MULTIPLE CHOICE. Circle the letter in front of the correct answer for each of the following questions.

1 New spiritual life, which begins when one experiences the new birth, resembles human infancy in which one of the following ways?
a) It is and will always be irresponsible for the way it develops and for what it becomes.
b) Spiritual life develops naturally without any conscious effort.
c) Spiritual life develops by chance; therefore, some make it, some don't.
d) It is subject to growth, development, and maturity.

2 Spiritual growth and vitality, which our Lord wills for His children, are related directly to the Christian's
a) desire to develop his spiritual life to the full.
b) spiritual nourishment, nurture, and exercise.
c) willingness to let the Spirit assume and maintain control of his life.
d) response to the things mentioned in b) and c) above.
e) response to the things noted in answers a), b), and c).

3 The nature of spiritual life, we have learned, is such that if it is to be experienced to the full, it must undergo
a) severe discipline, which indicates one's worthiness to be advanced spiritually.
b) growth and development which lead toward maturity.
c) many setbacks, lapses, and failures if it is to be worthwhile.
d) rapid change at the beginning and immediate and constant progress in maturity.

4 All of the following statements but one give reasons why spiritual growth is needed. Which one is NOT one of the reasons we discussed?
a) Spiritual growth and development are the normal expectation of what is spiritually alive.
b) The growth and development of spiritual life to full fruit-bearing potential is commanded by our Lord.
c) Spiritual development is needed to prevent spiritual boredom.
d) Spiritual development is part of a process of growth toward maturity which continues as long as it is nourished properly under the Spirit's control.

5 The nurture of spiritual life is vitally important because it
a) tends to be frail in its infancy and needs spiritual support to help gain stature and spiritual vitality.
b) can never be sustained without the help of many sympathetic people.
c) is impossible to understand without the assistance of spiritual specialists.
d) needs to be mediated by spiritually mature people who act as spokesmen between newborn Christians and God.

6 We have seen that nurture of spiritual life is needed so that new converts
a) will be able to make the transition more easily from the old life to their new way of living.
b) may not have to go through times of testing and hardship such as many older Christians have.
c) may become dependent on older believers for spiritual growth.
d) can survive spiritually and develop toward Christian maturity.

7 We are aware that various levels of spiritual life exist because (choose the best answer based on our discussion in this lesson)
a) spiritual life always follows biological life principles faithfully.
b) various degrees of rewards are placed before the aspiring Christian in the Word to motivate him to excel in good works.
c) Scripture gives us the diet that is compatible for each stage of spiritual development from spiritual infancy to spiritual maturity.

8 A mature Christian, according to biblical definition, is the person who
a) strives to excel in every spiritual enterprise.
b) through constant use of his spiritual faculties has learned to distinguish good from evil.
c) is molded by time into an honored vessel.
d) is supported by popular consent to lead people and to make decisions for them.

9 The man who has never begun to live spiritually is characterized in Scripture as one who
a) is potentially dead in sins and trespasses.
b) is able to respond very minimally to spiritual things.
c) cannot comprehend the issues of life in general.
d) cannot receive or understand spiritual truth.

10 The person described in Scripture as the worldly man exhibits what qualities?
a) He exists on a weak, spiritual diet, prefers evangelistic preaching to teaching on the deeper life, is often contentious, and enjoys the privileges of spiritual infancy.
b) He cannot apprehend spiritual truth, understand his spiritual responsibilities, decide to make spiritual changes in his life, and help himself or alter his situation.
c) He loves the things of the world: amusements, enterprises, associations, and acclaim.
d) He has determined to reject spiritual truth and the reproach associated with it in order to enjoy the friendship of the world.

11 The spiritual man is characterized by his
a) other-worldly attitude, avoidance of nonspiritual people, and the world in general.
b) rigid adherence to rules, regulations, and appearances: he seldom if ever leaves his church to mix with common people.
c) commitment to the Lord, ability to teach the truths of God's Word, and ability to discriminate between spiritual truth and error.
d) emaciated features, poor clothing, spare diet, and unkempt appearance.

12 Scripture indicates that the major difference among these levels of spirituality is
a) that of time and exposure to the Word of God.
b) the ability to receive and understand spiritual truth.
c) the type of person involved: some respond to truth; some do not.
d) one of degree only: the difference between the unspiritual man and the mature man is simply the amount of light each has received.

13 One's spiritual development is directly related to his
a) opportunities to attend church and learn its precepts.
b) environment: if it is favorable, he will develop rapidly; however, if it is unfavorable, he will develop slowly if at all.
c) background training in spiritual things.
d) response to the Word of God, which is a key building block of productive spiritual life.

14 Spiritual growth is nurtured through relationships because relationships
a) fill the role of active support one needs as he develops from spiritual infancy to spiritual maturity.
b) provide the basis for one's faith and conduct.
c) supplement the active role of the Word of God in developing character.
d) are the most important ingredient in building one's spiritual life.

15 According to this lesson, one element of spiritual growth which affects both the maturing believer and those less mature than he is
a) knowledge of spiritual responsibilities and what believers need to do.
b) the application of his knowledge: sharing with others and helping them to develop spiritually.
c) the ability to judge the productive efforts of others in order to show them how much they need to improve.
d) the ability to find the will of the Lord for other people, especially the immature.

answers to study questions

7 a without the spirit. Your answer may differ a bit from mine. I've noted that never having been born again, this man did not comprehend or respond to the Spirit. He was trying to apprehend God's truth on a nonspiritual basis, and it did not change him.

b worldly. I've noted that they are spiritual infants who still savor the simple (milk) diet and their relative freedom from responsibility. They evidence worldliness in their lack of commitment to hear and apply the truth and thus grow spiritually.

c spiritual. I've noted that Dan obviously understands his Christian responsibilities and has clearly assumed them. He gives evidence of a growing relationship with the Lord. He is no longer a learner of basic truths, but a teacher of others. As a result, his own spiritual life is growing and maturing in spite of adversity.

1 a False.
b False.
c True.
d True.
e True.

8 You should have circled answers a), b), and c). Answer d) is incorrect, for spiritual life is not encouraged by simple mental assent. Bible truth works to change not only the mind but also the behavior of an individual.

2 b) grow and develop toward maturity.

9 a False.
b True.
c True.
d False. (As one abides in Christ and is responsive to the Spirit's control, he grows; however, this is not a purely automatic process. God initiates but we must respond for growth to occur.)

3 c) enables one to accomplish successfully the Lord's purpose.

10 a) Bob attends church regularly and studies the Word consistently.

4 a False.
  b True.
  c True.
  d False.

11 You should have circled answers b), c), and d). Answer a) is not right because spiritual growth takes more than knowledge; it requires one to apply that knowledge to his life.

5 a Milk and solid food.
  b milk, solid food
  c distinguish good from evil, works of service, unity in the faith, the whole measure of Christ.

12 a 2) Doesn't promote maturity.
  b 1) Promotes maturity.
  c 1) Promotes maturity.
  d 2) Doesn't promote maturity.
  e 1) Promotes maturity.
  f 1) Promotes maturity.

6 a 2) The worldly man.
  b 1) Man without the Spirit.
  c 3) The spiritual man.
  d 1) Man without the Spirit.
  e 2) The worldly man.
  f 3) The spiritual man.

LESSON 2

Toward Maturity

Juan and Maria quickly adjusted to having a new member in their family. They felt happy as the various friends and family members came to visit little Manuel. "Oh, he looks just like his daddy," different ones commented, causing Juan to feel particularly proud. Maria also saw a resemblance between the father and his son. She and Juan compared Manuel's baby photo with some that Juan's mother had kept when Juan was a baby. There could be no mistaking, there was a very definite similarity.

You may have had a similar experience. Someone may have remarked about how much you look like one of your family ancestors. It can be an enjoyable experience to look back through an old photo album and observe the physical likenesses of different members of a family, even across several generations.

It should not surprise you then to discover in this lesson that the Christian life also includes some "look-alikes." Jesus has given us His life. Wouldn't you expect that as converts grow toward spiritual maturity there would be an increasing revelation of His life? In this lesson you will discover that the ultimate goal of spiritual growth is to develop Christlikeness. You will also learn what the Bible teaches

about some of the elements involved in this process. What you learn in this lesson will prove valuable as you help others grow toward spiritual maturity.

lesson outline

Into His Likeness
Making Persons Whole
Step by Step

lesson objectives

After studying this lesson you should be able:

■ Explain the goal of spiritual growth.

■ Identify the role of Christian nurture in developing the whole life of Christians.

■ Discuss the process by which one moves from spiritual infancy to spiritual maturity.

learning activities

1. Study the lesson according to the instructions given in the learning activities in Lesson 1. Be sure to read all Scripture texts given and answer each study question before looking at the answer we have given at the end of the lesson.

2. Look in the glossary at the end of the study guide for definitions of key words you do not know. Understanding the meaning of these words is necessary so that you will understand the lesson content.

3. Take the self-test and check your answers with those we have given at the end of the study guide.

key words

capabilities	ethical	orientation
concepts	exemplary	predestined
conform	indeterminate	responsive
developmental	innate	transformation
distinctive	instantaneous	ultimate
distorted	integration	values
edification	motives	

lesson development

INTO HIS LIKENESS

Spiritual Development Expected

Objective 1. *Select statements which explain correctly why it is natural for Christians to develop in Christlikeness.*

All life has a nature distinctive to its own kind. The character of that life is transmitted through the processes of reproduction. A seed is alive. Given the proper conditions for growth, the character of that life will be revealed. When you plant a grain of rice, corn,

42

beans, or anything else, you know what will grow from it. The distinctive nature of the life is contained in the seed. Under appropriate conditions, the character of that life will burst forth and develop to fullness.

This truth is important to recognize when considering spiritual life. The *new life* God gives in Jesus is His own life. His life, too, has its own distinctive nature and character. As the *new life* is nurtured under proper spiritual conditions it grows and develops within us, and we become more and more like Him. Our responsibility is to be sensitive to the Holy Spirit, permitting Him to control and shape our new life according to His will (Romans 8:5-11; Galatians 5:25).

1 Circle the letter in front of each TRUE statement.
a When nurtured properly, the Christian life will develop into Christlikeness.
b One's spiritual life will develop automatically once it has begun.
c Our responsibility in developing spiritual life is to respond to the work of the Holy Spirit.
d Christlikeness is the normal expectation of the new life.
e The kind of life God gives us determines what grows from it.

Spiritual Development Is God's Purpose

Objective 2. *Choose statements which explain the effect of the Fall and God's purpose in man's salvation.*

In Genesis 1:26-27 we observe that man was originally created in God's image and likeness. Man was made by God and he was made *like* God. He was everything God wanted him to be. But this likeness to God was severely marred when he fell into sin. He became an unholy creature and the image of God in him was seriously distorted. God's activity in salvation concerns His plan to bring man back into his original condition in the likeness of God. God warned man that sin would bring death, separation from Him. When man sinned, he died spiritually. But in Jesus we are given new life, we become alive spiritually. As that life grows and develops within, we begin the process of becoming increasingly like Him.

2-3 Circle the letter of the correct answer for each question.

2 What affect did the Fall have on man's original likeness to God?
a) It remained intact.
b) It was marred by sin.
c) It has improved through the centuries.
d) We don't know.

3 What is God's purpose in man's salvation?
a) To leave him alone
b) To make him miserable in his sin
c) To prove that he was wrong
d) To restore him to God's likeness

The Goal of Spiritual Development

Objective 3. *Identify the correct description of what God has determined for those who receive new life in Christ.*

Scripture indicates that God, in His eternal plan, has predetermined the outcome of those who receive His new life. God knows what we will be like once His work in us is completed.

4 Read Romans 8:28-29 and answer the following question. To what are those who receive new life in Jesus predestined?

....

You should understand here that it is God's intention that those who receive His life will grow and develop. As they grow, the nature and character of God will be revealed in them and the likeness of Christ will be seen in their conversations, actions, and habits. Peter refers to this developmental process when he admonishes those with new life to "grow in the grace and knowledge of our Lord Jesus Christ" (2 Peter 3:18).

5 God has determined that those who receive new life in Christ are to become
a) equal to the angels in character, privilege, and glory.
b) a new humanity equal to divinity in every way.
c) progressively changed into the likeness of the Son of God.
d) perfect through an instantaneous experience sometime in their life.

6 What does Scripture mean by the term *become mature*?
a) To attain the whole measure of Christlikeness
b) To attend church services regularly
c) To discontinue certain social practices
d) To disassociate oneself from the physical world

I once heard two boys playing together. They were discussing which one of them was bigger. Soon they stood up back to back with each other. Each stretched as much as he could, and they rubbed their hands over the tops of their heads to see which was the taller. One boy was delighted to prove he was the taller. But the other boy didn't give up so easily. He said, "Just wait. When you get to be as big as your dad, and I get to be as big as my dad, then I'll be bigger than you." This boy grasped an important truth. He saw the prospects of growth. He had adopted a model he wanted to grow up to be like: his father. This illustrates what it means to attain the whole measure of all that Christ is.

Periodically we do well to stand back to back with Jesus—to take spiritual inventory. While He may measure bigger and taller than we do, each time we measure ourselves by this standard we should see growth. We should be more like Him.

The Task of Christian Nurture

Objective 4. *Explain the task of Christian nurture.*

The goal of spiritual growth is for Christians to mature into the likeness of Jesus. As we allow the life of Christ within us to develop fully, we will become increasingly more Christlike. Because of the life of Jesus within us, we mature into His likeness, allowing His life to be perfected in us.

The task of those who would nurture Christian growth is to supply what is needed for normal, healthy spiritual growth. Nurturing Christian growth concerns life—with helping Christians grow in the Christ-life until His nature and character are revealed in their personalities.

The goal of mature Christians is not merely to produce people who possess unlimited Bible knowledge and spiritual insights, but to help them live the new life to the fullest, as Jesus intended it to be. The object of Christian nurture is to help people exemplify Jesus—to lead them into disciplined, growing lives in God with Jesus as the center of focus.

Whenever you engage in helping people grow spiritually and develop in Christlikeness, you are engaging in Christian nurture. This is a rewarding, practical ministry which is deeply anchored in God's design for mankind.

7 Circle the letter in front of the completion which explains best the task of the Christian nurture as defined in this section. The task of Christian nurture is helping people to
a) gain some basic Bible knowledge.
b) grow spiritually and to live life to the fullest.
c) acquire deep spiritual insight and become experts in the Law.
d) discriminate between right and wrong behavior in their respective cultures.

MAKING PERSONS WHOLE

The Christ-Centered Life

Objective 5. *State who is to be the center of the Christian life.*

Christian nurture concerns life because Christianity is centered in life. Christianity revolves around Christ, a person, the eternal Son of God, who is the source of all life. He gives His life to those who receive Him. Commitment to Jesus Christ begins with a response in simple faith to the gospel. This marks the beginning of new life. But this commitment involves a life of discipleship through the process of growth toward Christlikeness. In this process of spiritual birth and growth Jesus is, and increasingly becomes, the center of the Christian's total life experience. Through Christian nurture growing Christians learn how to put Christ first in their lives, making Him the center of their whole lives.

8 The Christian life is centered around

....

What the Christ-Centered Life Is

Objective 6. *Explain what it means to make Jesus central in our lives.*

Helping people make Jesus the center of their lives touches every aspect of human experience. When we think about the human person, we sometimes tend to divide the person into parts or areas of life, such as the mental area, the physical area, the emotional area, the social area, and the spiritual area. While it is helpful to study human behavior from these different points of view, we need to remember that persons are whole beings and they cannot be divided into small parts. Every area of life affects others and we respond to our surroundings as whole persons.

The Christian's relationship to God through Jesus affects every part of the person. Christ is at the center and that means He should control every area. The more we grow spiritually and take on His likeness, the more He controls all of our lives.

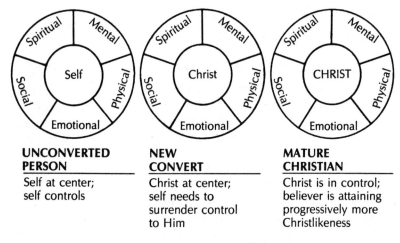

UNCONVERTED PERSON	NEW CONVERT	MATURE CHRISTIAN
Self at center; self controls	Christ at center; self needs to surrender control to Him	Christ is in control; believer is attaining progressively more Christlikeness

9 Circle the letter in front of each TRUE statement.

a Each area of human life acts independently of all other ones.

b The Christian's relationship to God affects every part of life.

c Helping people make Jesus the center of their lives includes every area of the human life.

d The more Christians grow spiritually, the more Jesus controls their lives.

e As Christians mature, their lives become more divided into distinct parts.

The Role of Christian Nurture in Developing Whole Persons

Objective 7. *Choose a statement which describes how Christian nurture seeks to make a person whole in Jesus.*

The object of Christian nurture is to develop whole mature persons: persons who are intellectually, emotionally, spiritually, and socially changed through their relationship with Jesus Christ.

Those concerned with Christian nurture recognize the innate worth of each person, perceive the potential within every human being, and seek to develop this is to the fullest for God's glory. Christian nurture is concerned about the whole life of Christians and seeks to help them be whole and live life to the full.

This concern for making persons whole in Jesus leads to a discipleship which is expressed in total obedience to everything Jesus commanded. The faith-response to the gospel leads to an active, obedient love for the Lord Jesus. This is a love from the whole person—heart, mind, and soul—which yields control of all life to Him.

10 All of the following statements but one describe correctly how Christian nurture seeks to make persons whole in Jesus. Which one is NOT correct? Christian nurture seeks to develop the
a) intellectual potential of every believer.
b) emotional and spiritual capabilities of believers.
c) social potential of each believer.
d) political skills and competence of believers.
e) spiritual capacities of believers.

11 If you agree that the role of Christian nurture is to produce whole persons, how will this affect your Christian nurture task? Write your answer in your notebook.

The Role of the Bible in Developing Whole Persons

Objective 8. *Explain how the Bible contributes to making persons whole.*

In Lesson 1 you were introduced to the way the Bible helps nurture spiritual growth. God reveals Himself in the Scriptures; therefore, they are the content of our study and learning. We want to become Christlike and He is revealed in the Word of God. We do not study the Bible merely to gain knowledge for its own sake. The purpose of our learning is not to prepare to pass an examination but to prepare to live whole, Christ-centered lives.

The truth of God took on living expression in Jesus Christ. Since His life is within us, God should take on living expression in our lives. The Christian's total personality is to be transformed by the reality of God within so that the Christian's life is a faithful expression of the truth of God. As the Christian life grows within, there should be a progressive transformation of the Christian's character, values, motives, attitudes, and conduct to conform to the personality of God as expressed in Jesus. Christians should become increasingly more Christlike.

Second Timothy 3:14-17 identifies four uses of Scripture: teaching, rebuking, correcting, and training in righteousness. Also notice that these four activities have one basic goal: the equipping of the man of God for every good work. The Scriptures are useful in preparing Christians to experience all that God wants them to become; we could say that the Scriptures are useful for making persons whole. If you want to grow spiritually, you should study the Scriptures; if you want to help someone else mature spiritually, you should help him study the Bible.

12 Circle the letter of each TRUE statement.
a The Bible contributes toward making persons whole because it provides the formula, as well as the measure, for spiritual growth.
b The Bible places definite limits on spiritual growth and development.
c The Bible reveals God's will for spiritual development and gives specific guidelines that will result in making persons whole.
d The Bible presents a model of the truly whole person in Jesus, who is to be our pattern.
e The goal of our Bible study is to develop a broad base of knowledge so that we can demonstrate our spirituality to others.

Let's review and summarize what you have studied so far in this lesson. You have discovered that maturing Christians are growing in Christlikeness. It is God's intention that those who receive new life in Christ mature so that the life of Jesus is increasingly revealed in them. You have also learned that maturity in the Christ-life involves becoming whole persons, yielding to His control in every area of life. You have learned that helping persons become whole, that is, Christlike, is the main task of those involved in Christian nurture. And you have learned that the Bible is essential to helping persons become whole. If you do not yet understand these concepts, review what you have already studied in this lesson before you proceed to the next section.

STEP BY STEP

The Goal of Christian Nurture

Objective 9. *Differentiate between intermediate goals and the ultimate goal of Christian nurture.*

When a baby is born, he begins to grow. We expect the ultimate outcome of that growth to be adulthood—maturity. We recognize that the process of growth from infancy to adulthood takes time and patience. We have learned to recognize stages of development and levels of maturity. At each stage of development we expect the growing person to perform certain tasks, such as learning to walk in early childhood. The performances we expect at each stage of development are referred to as *intermediate goals*. They represent smaller objectives toward which one works enroute to the ultimate goal of adulthood—maturity. Each of these intermediate objectives is worthwhile by itself, but each one is even more significant when it is viewed as a step toward the *ultimate goal*. Understanding this concept helps us take better care of developing people's needs. As the needs of each developmental level are met, we are helping the individual grow toward maturity.

13 Read 1 Corinthians 3:1-4 and 1:10-12 and compare these Scripture references with 1 Corinthians 1:2-9. Based upon the preceding section and the foregoing Scripture references, how can we justify Paul's use of words such as *sanctified, holy,* and *grace* when referring to people who had so many problems? Use your notebook for this answer.

Spiritual life, once again, parallels the growth and development process in biological life. The maturing process initiated by the new birth begins with spiritual infancy. The ultimate goal of the believer's spiritual life is to be transformed into the likeness of Christ (Romans 8:29; 12:2; 2 Corinthians 3:18). As he begins his spiritual journey, he needs nourishment that will produce sound growth. He must develop a taste for the milk of the Word (1 Peter 2:2). He thus

51

learns basic requirements for wholesome spiritual development according to God's design. He learns to perform the tasks and demonstrate the behavior expected for his initial stage of development. He is, so to speak, *learning to walk*. As he develops an appetite for the Word and learns to apply its directions to his daily life, his faith grows. He learns the nature of spiritual warfare by perusing the Word (Ephesians 6:10, 18) and by experience—through personal encounters with the enemy of his soul. As he relates to more mature believers, he learns that the secret of successful spiritual combat comes through prayer. His stature thus increases as he journeys onward, growing in the Word, his relationship with the Lord, and with fellow believers. Progressively, he takes on the image of Christ as he moves toward his ultimate goal. Developing a taste for the Word, engaging in consistent prayer, learning to discern truth and error—these are not learned all at once. Each bit of stature gained is an intermediate goal, but it is part of the overall or ultimate goal of developing Christlikeness.

Read the following summary definition through several times and commit it to memory. You will be required to demonstrate your knowledge of this definition on the self-test, as well as in the student report. More important, however, you will have a clear understanding of the ultimate goal of Christian nurture.

> The ultimate goal of Christian nurture is to cultivate spiritual growth toward mature Christlikeness in all of life's experiences.

14 In differentiating between intermediate goals and the ultimate goal of Christian nurture, we can say most accurately that intermediate goals are
a) relatively unimportant parts of the ultimate goal.
b) important as ends in themselves.
c) smaller objectives to be reached en route to the ultimate goal.
d) the goals of individuals; whereas, the institution holds the ultimate goal.

15 In the following exercise write a 1) in front of each statement which gives an intermediate goal of Christian nurture and a 2) in front of those that represent the ultimate goal of Christian nurture.

.... **a** Teach the new believer to read the Word of God and to base his life on its teachings.

.... **b** Teach believers the principles of spiritual growth that can change every aspect of their lives progressively into the image of Christ.

.... **c** Teach the aspiring Christian principles of effective praying and how it helps build spiritual stature.

.... **d** Inspire believers to aspire toward spiritual wholeness so that when they stand before Christ they will be fully mature and lack nothing in Him.

.... **e** Teach believers the necessity of assembling together for the mutual edification of themselves individually and the body collectively.

Steps Toward Spiritual Maturity

Objective 10. *List six needs to be met en route to the ultimate goal of Christlikeness.*

Read Ephesians 4:11-16. You read verse 13 earlier in this lesson. This passage indicates that growing Christians are to measure to the fullness of Christ. It also teaches that the mature Christian will properly identify himself with the body of Christ, the local congregation of believers, and will take an active role in the ministry of that body. With this idea in mind, what steps or needs can be identified? Beginning with receiving new life in Christ, spiritual birth, and progressing toward full spiritual maturity, what tasks need to be achieved en route?

16 In your notebook write a list of steps you think a convert should take between spiritual infancy and spiritual maturity.

In question number **16**, I asked you to list what you think, so there can be no right or wrong answers. Here are six steps I think are important following the reception of new life in Christ:

1. Orientation to living the new life
2. Integration into a fellowship of believers
3. Development of spiritual life
4. Discover spiritual ministry gifts
5. Equipping for Christian service
6. Active involvement in Christian service

It helps me to think of these steps as a cycle which repeats itself. As you receive new life and develop to the point of active involvement in Christian service, others are led to receive new life and the process begins again. The following model pictures this cycle:

EVANGELISM PRODUCES

0. New life in Christ

6. Active involvement in Christian service

1. Orientation to new life

5. Equipping for Christian service

2. Integration into fellowship of believers

4. Discovery of spiritual ministry gifts

3. Development of spiritual life

A MODEL FOR SPIRITUAL LIFE DEVELOPMENT
(A Pattern for the Christian Nurturing Ministry)

17 In your notebook write this list several times and review it until you can list these six steps in the order given. You can use this list as a general guide to determine at what stage of development a person is. Remember: The process of maturing is progressive; therefore, the stages tend to blend from one level to another. These six steps represent realistic categories that will help you plan Christian nurturing activities intelligently for those you are helping to grow spiritually. Using these steps you can move people from their present levels to the next higher levels and on toward active involvement as mature Christians.

Six Need Levels

Objective 11. *Identify each of the six need levels required for spiritual life development.*

To use these six levels of development to help someone grow spiritually, you need to be able not only to list them but also to understand them well enough to describe them.

1. *Orientation to living the new life.* We have already observed the need for this. Babes need to be fed milk until they mature sufficiently so that they can receive stronger food. The person who becomes a Christian undergoes a whole change in way of life, attitudes, and values. Often he needs assurance of salvation and he needs to receive the careful, basic, elementary learning that starts him in the direction of development toward spiritual maturity. Often this orientation prepares the new Christian to declare his faith in the Christian rite of water baptism.

2. *Integration into a fellowship of believers.* Because Christians are people who share the new life God gives in Jesus, they are related to each other. All Christians are part of one body—the body of Christ. This body of Christ is expressed on earth in local fellowships of believers. The believer cannot mature properly without the relationships of this body; consequently, the body needs each individual to contribute his strengths and gifts for the body to be whole.

3. *Development of spiritual life.* Just as a person must eat throughout the entirety of his life, so the new life needs continual nurture. As you have already discovered, this results from receiving more and more of God's Word. A Christian never outgrows his need for receiving more spiritual food. He does, however, find himself able to receive stronger food as he grows. At this stage the believer discovers the value of personal Bible study and prayer. He begins to sharpen his critical thinking skills as he compares Scripture with Scripture and the doctrine he hears taught or preached with the Bible standard.

4. *Discovery of spiritual ministry gifts.* God has given every Christian a gift or ability for ministry. It is important that each Christian exercise his gift in ministry. In this way the Christian himself and the body of which he is a part develop to wholeness. Some Christians have not yet discovered their ministry gift. They wonder what abilities they have which would minister to others. These people need to analyze their activities and decide which ones seem to be a blessing and help to others in the Body of Christ. They need to examine their hearts to see which activities bring them a sense of satisfaction and joy. By doing this, they will have an indication of their special ministry gift(s).

5. *Equipping for Christian service.* Once a person has discovered his ministry gift, he needs to develop it. At this stage of development, one should be available to do whatever tasks are needed in terms of body ministry. On a personal level, also, one should do everything possible to learn how he may develop and use his gift in service to his family, friends, acquaintances, and community. Being trained for Christian service shows a willingness to do what God wants to promote spiritual growth, and it implies a high degree of spiritual maturity.

6. *Active involvement in Christian service.* Receiving training for Christian service is valuable; however, it can be effective only if it is used in active involvement in the Lord's work. Discovering opportunities for Christian service and using those opportunities for actual service for God are essential.

18 Match the name of each need level (right) with its appropriate description (left).

....**a** Must be incorporated into the body of believers; is strengthened by the body and adds fresh vision and vitality

....**b** Must be challenged to identify the specific talent God has given him

....**c** Must be encouraged to discover and use opportunities to do the work of the Lord

....**d** Must develop the specific gift or gifts with which God has endowed him for service

....**e** Must be taught concerning Christian attitudes, values; needs reassurance of salvation

....**f** Must be encouraged to evaluate the truths of God's Word, pray, and cultivate spiritual capacity

1) Orientation to new life
2) Integration into fellowship
3) Development of spiritual life
4) Discovery of gifts
5) Equipping for service
6) Involvement in service

Christian Needs and Spiritual Maturity

Objective 12. *Choose a statement that explains how the six steps which lead toward spiritual maturity relate to Christian nurture.*

You have discovered that the ultimate goal of Christian nurture is to cultivate spiritual growth toward Christlikeness in the whole of life's experiences. You have also discovered six needs to be met en route to this ultimate goal. Christian nurture should take these need levels into account and provide opportunities to help people grow from one level to another. Whatever the level of development, the ultimate goal should always be in focus. We, then, can think of these six levels of needs as *en route objectives* for our work in Christian nurturing.

19 The six steps which lead toward spiritual maturity relate to Christian education in the following way:
a) They are the center of focus and are the same as the ultimate goal.
b) They are intermediate objectives which must be met en route to the ultimate goal.
c) They may be used instead of the ultimate goal by those who are less gifted or motivated.
d) They are ideals which need not be met as long as we keep the ultimate goal in focus.

self-test

MULTIPLE CHOICE. Circle the letter in front of the correct answer for each of the following questions.

1 Spiritual growth is a process which has as its ultimate goal the
a) development of model citizens in each community.
b) progressive development of Christlikeness in each believer.
c) development of the believer's social conscience.
d) change of believers from spiritual infancy to maturity by means of self-determination.

2 Spiritual growth involves the renewal in man of
a) his original likeness of God.
b) the potential for growth his earlier ancestors possessed.
c) the potential for immediate spiritual perfection.
d) an intellectual capability of understanding more about God.

3 Which statement most accurately describes the relationship between spiritual maturity and Christlikeness?
a) Spiritual maturity relates to time; Christlikeness relates to eternity.
b) Spiritual maturity precedes Christlikeness, which develops more slowly.
c) Spiritual maturity means to attain to the full measure of Christlikeness.
d) Spiritual maturity is characterized by imperfection; Christlikeness is equated with perfection.

4 The nurturing task of Christian nurture primarily is helping people to
a) develop appropriate ethical standards.
b) become sensitive to various kinds of acceptable worship.
c) have an adequate understanding of Bible knowledge.
d) grow spiritually.

5 The role of Christian nurture in developing whole persons is best described as one which seeks to
a) encourage each person to recognize his own worth.
b) motivate individuals to good works to demonstrate their faith.
c) develop the full potential of each person for God's glory.
d) create in each person the capacity for positive thinking and action.

6 The main task of Christian nurture is to help people become whole—that is, to
a) become Christlike.
b) be fully developed as natural human beings.
c) be aware of their perfectibility.
d) realize the limited nature of their potential but to develop this to the fullest extent.

7 Considering the process of developing our new life in Christ to spiritual maturity, we realize that
a) the process of development is hard to define since the stages are so indeterminate.
b) the task of Christian nurture is difficult, since each person's spiritual development is unique to him.
c) each stage in development requires a fixed amount of time, if development is to be complete.
d) there are stages of development and levels of maturity.

8 All of the following statements but one reveal the needs which must be met en route to the goal of Christlikeness. Which one does NOT represent these needs?
a) Orientation to new life and integration into a body of believers
b) Development of spiritual life and discovery of spiritual gifts
c) Realization of spiritual potential and development of whole self-concept
d) Equipping for and active involvement in Christian service

9 The ultimate goal of Christian nurture as presented in this lesson, is to
a) nurture the new believer until he becomes mature enough to stand alone.
b) nurture spiritual growth, in the whole of life's experience, toward maturity expressed in Christlikeness.
c) strive to produce whole individuals who are blameless in thought, word, and deed.
d) carry out the biblical command to "teach all nations."

10 The six steps identified in this lesson as *need levels* are considered as
a) mechanical devices which are established to help set up the Christian nurture program.
b) more or less arbitrary statements which describe the developmental process of spiritual life.
c) lower level objectives that may represent the ultimate goal for some people.
d) en route enablement that helps one move from infancy to the ultimate goal of spiritual maturity.

answers to study questions

10 d) political skills and competence of believers.

1 a True.
 b False.
 c True.
 d True.
 e True.

11 Your answer. You probably noted that you will be required to broaden your efforts to help minister to the total person. Those who have received new life in Jesus should develop into better citizens, better neighbors, better husbands, wifes, children, or parents. They should be better employees or employers, as the case may be. They will be more enlightened and compassionate as they develop into the whole persons their Lord wills them to be. At this point they will be much more conscientious about fulfilling their spiritual responsibilities than when they were just beginning their new life.

2 b) It was marred by sin.

12 a True.
b False.
c True.
d True.
e False.

3 d) To restore him to God's likeness.

13 Your answer should include the ideas I've suggested. Paul notes that the Corinthians are called to be holy. The new birth has sanctified them, that is, set them apart unto God. Their behavior demonstrates the grace of God that has so dramatically changed them (cf. 1 Corinthians 6:9-11). They have not become instantly perfect human beings, however. In their spiritual infancy they demonstrate *childish behavior*. In this milk-diet stage, they must be taught basic doctrines and handled with love, patience, and care. As they grow in grace and understanding, they will partake of stronger meat, an adult diet, of more advanced knowledge. They are called to be saints; the apostle encourages them to be what they are.

4 Those who receive new life are predestined to be conformed to His likeness.

14 c) smaller objectives to be reached en route to the ultimate goal.

5 c) progressively changed into the likeness of the Son of God.

15 a 1) Intermediate goal.
b 1) Intermediate goal.
c 1) Intermediate goal.
d 2) Ultimate goal.
e 2) Ultimate goal.

6 a) To attain the whole measure of Christlikeness.

16 Your answer.

7 b) grow spiritually and to live life to the fullest.

17 Memorizing these steps now will enable you to do subsequent exercises more readily.

8 Jesus Christ.

18 a 2) Integration into fellowship.
  b 4) Discovery of gifts.
  c 6) Involvement in service.
  d 5) Equipping for service.
  e 1) Orientation to new life.
  f 3) Development of spiritual life.

9 a False.
  b True.
  c True.
  d True.
  e False.

19 b) They are intermediate objectives which must be met en route to the ultimate goal.

LESSON 3

Helping Christians Grow

Juan wondered how Maria always seemed to know just what little Manuel needed and how to provide the right care for his needs. Maria showed Juan a book on infant care written by a noted specialist at the university hospital. Her mother had purchased it for her while they waited for Manuel's arrival. The book discussed many of the things a new mother needed to know. Maria also explained that she had spent many hours watching her mother care for her younger brother and sister. Sometimes she babysat with them while her mother was away. Thus, Maria learned how to care for a baby from the experiences of others who shared with her and from her own experience.

Christians need to learn how to nurture spiritual growth—how to promote the spiritual development of others. The Bible reveals a divine method and some divine resources to help achieve the task.

In this lesson you will learn that disciple-making is the divine method for nurturing young believers, and you will discover that the divine resources include the nature of the church, the ministry gifts, and the Holy Spirit. You will also discover that there are informal and formal patterns of nurturing spiritual growth. As you become involved in the task of disciple-making and utilize the resources God has placed at your disposal, you will see lives changed

gloriously: those you are helping to grow and your own as well. Such is the benefit of nurturing spiritual growth.

lesson outline

A Divine Method
Some Divine Resources
Patterns of Nurturing Spiritual Growth

lesson objectives

When you finish this lesson you should be able to:

- Recognize explanations which show how the biblical concept of disciple-making relates to nurturing spiritual growth.

- Identify statements that explain how the nature of the church, ministry gifts, and the ministry of the Holy Spirit relate to nurturing spiritual growth.

- Distinguish between examples of informal and formal patterns of nurturing spiritual growth.

learning activities

1. Study the lesson following the study plan given in the learning activities for Lessons 1 and 2.

2. Take the self-test and check your answers with those we have given at the end of the study guide.

3. Carefully review Unit 1 (Lessons 1-3), then complete the unit student report for Unit 1 and send it to your ICI instructor.

key words

adherent	imbibe	revelatory process
emulate	imitation	sympathetic
expertise	incentive	technique
hierarchy	interdependent	unique
identification	mimic	vocabularies

lesson development

A DIVINE METHOD

Christians are alive and growing toward full spiritual maturity which is defined as Christlikeness. The task of the church collectively and of maturing Christians individually is to help Christians grow spiritually. You may wonder how to do this. You have learned that growth is natural and expected; yet there are conditions favorable to proper growth. In helping Christians grow, we need to learn how to arrange the conditions to facilitate the natural tendency toward growth. The Bible reveals a divine method called disciple-making.

What a Disciple Is

Objective 1. *Select statements which describe what a disciple is and what is the goal of Christian nurture.*

Sometimes a disciple is thought of as a "follower", as one who follows the teaching of another. The word *disciple*, as it is used in the New Testament, literally means "learner"; however, more is implied than simply being a pupil. The term disciple implies a relationship with another person. Thus, one is a disciple in relationship with a teacher. It is possible for a learner to be guided by a teacher without embracing the teacher's conclusions and values. But this is not so with a disciple. A disciple learns from the teacher and comes to share his teacher's attitudes, actions, and values. A disciple becomes an adherent of the teacher. He has a devotion to the teacher and desires to become like him. A disciple seeks to imitate the teacher, to mimic what he sees the teacher do or understands him to believe. So one is a disciple when he binds himself to another to acquire the theoretical or practical knowledge that his model displays. The view of the disciple-teacher relationship is perceived correctly as an *informal relationship* involving two people: the one living and acting as a model and the other seeking to emulate his example. It is not the same as the *formal relationship* which exists between a student and his professor.

An apprentice in a trade serves as an appropriate example of what a disciple is. The master craftsman has learned a trade from another who has taught him. He has developed his skills in the trade under the watchful supervision of the master until he has acquired the expertise that sets him apart as a master. When a person does not have these skills but desires to learn the trade, he joins himself to a master craftsman for some time. He learns by observing the master craftsman and applying what he has observed. He strives to imitate the skill of the master, and thus he develops his own technique and skills in the trade. In doing so, the apprentice tends to become like the master who teaches him. He follows the master craftsman's instructional example, and in the faithful application of his knowledge he becomes like the master. The apprentice learns from the master craftsman by following him, by imitating him.

In a sense, the process of disciple-making resembles the development of an apprentice. Because of the nature of their relationship, we can imagine that the apprentice increasingly takes on the characteristics of the master who teaches him. By associating with and by imitating the master, the apprentice learns the style, skills, and knowledge of the master. Similarly, a disciple conforms to the likeness of his teacher. Because Christians are becoming Christlike, they are considered to be disciples of Jesus.

Learned men in ancient times often maintained a group of disciples. Usually these disciples were young learners who associated closely with the scholars to learn from them as well as perhaps to serve their physical needs. The relationship between Eli and Samuel may be understood in this way (1 Samuel 1:21-28; 3:1). Ancient Greek philosophers, such as Socrates, had disciples, and the Jewish rabbis likewise had their adherents. John the Baptist was surrounded by a group of disciples and so was Jesus. In each case, these disciples were bound to the teacher to learn from him, follow his teachings, and imitate him. In a word, they were to become like the teacher.

1 Circle the letter in front of each TRUE statement.
a The term *learner* fully describes the word *disciple*.
b The term *disciple* implies a relationship with another person.
c The disciple-teacher connection exists primarily on a formal level.
d The teacher becomes the disciple's model in terms of attitudes, actions, and values.

2 The process of disciple-making is similar to that which an apprentice undergoes as he seeks to become a master
a) because in both cases the one who receives training can be effective only after many years of training.
b) in that the disciple learns by observing, being with, and doing the teacher's bidding.
c) because the nature of both relationships is formal and is characterized by exacting standards.

The ultimate goal of Christian nurture is to help Christians mature spiritually toward Christlikeness. Another way to state the same thing is to say that the goal of Christian nurture is to make disciples. It is essential to remember that the intended goal is Christlikeness, not my likeness nor your likeness. It is the life of Christ within that is to be matured into a full expression of Christlikeness. The apostle Paul undoubtedly had this in mind when he admonished Philippian Christians to emulate the attitude and spirit of Christ as He addressed Himself to His redemptive purpose (Philippians 2:5-11).

This fact may be particularly important if you ever find yourself working with people of a culture different from your own. Your goal will not be to lead these people to become like you by adopting all of your cultural ways and values. Instead, your goal will be to lead them to be like Christ as expressed within their own cultural setting.

3 Circle the letter in front of each TRUE statement.

a More mature (and maturing) Christians strive to help other Christians mature spiritually toward Christlikeness.

b The goal of Christian nurturing is to produce sinless human beings who alone can bring glory to God through their superior knowledge.

c Leading disciples toward Christlikeness, the goal of Christian nurturing, means that Christians everywhere will share the same cultural standards and values.

d The Scriptures admonish Christians to be models of Christlikeness so that non-Christians and new Christians can see the practical expression of the Christ life in practicing Christians.

How Jesus Made Disciples

Objective 2. *Choose a statement which describes correctly how Jesus made disciples.*

Through His public teaching and because of the miracles He performed, multitudes followed Jesus and were called His disciples. They followed His teaching, continually learning from Him. From among these Jesus chose twelve men to enter into a very special relationship with Him. His intention was to make them into apostles—sent out ones. He planned to equip these twelve men as leaders and then send them out to continue the disciple-making work He had begun. This unique relationship continued with the Twelve until Jesus endued them with His Spirit and sent them forth into the world to preach His gospel. We can learn valuable lessons about the importance of the teacher-pupil relationship in disciple-making by observing the example of Jesus as He taught the Twelve.

4 Circle the letter of the best answer based upon the lesson content in this section. The method of disciple-making which Jesus employed was

a) that of choosing selectively from among the multitude of would-be followers to get those who were willing to make a total commitment to Him from the beginning.

b) one of recruiting many potential disciples and then eliminating those who did not demonstrate complete dedication to His cause.

c) that of appealing to many for commitment through His public teaching ministry and miraculous works, and on a more restricted level, training a smaller number of disciples to become master disciple-makers.

Choosing the Twelve

Objective 3. *Identify statements from a list of possible alternatives which indicate reasons why Jesus chose the Twelve and, specifically, why He wanted the Twelve to be with Him.*

Jesus chose the Twelve so that He could equip and send them out in His service. His plan was to disciple them and then send them out to make disciples of others.

Read Mark 3:14 carefully. Two facts are significant in this context: Jesus called the Twelve *first* to be with Him and *second* to send them out in ministry. He wanted to equip them for a life of service for Him. To provide this equipping, He used the discipling method. They would be with Him—enter into a special relationship with Him. They would learn from Him by associating with Him, observing Him, and applying the principles He taught. But the special, close relationship was not the whole objective. The intimate relationship, fulfilling as it was, was the chosen means to the end. The end was equipping for service.

Being With Him

Jesus' reasons for choosing the Twelve to be with Him reflects His goal for them. His goal was not to communicate knowledge alone. Instead, He sought to communicate likeness. Jesus believed that a fully trained person would become like his teacher (Luke 6:40). The word in the original language of the New Testament (koine Greek) that is translated "fully trained" in this verse means to complete thoroughly or to make complete. It thus carries the idea of making people complete or whole. Therefore, Jesus is saying, "When one has been made complete, he will be like his teacher."

The making of a disciple of Jesus focuses on making one a complete person, a mature believer. Jesus knew that the way to achieve this end was to bring the Twelve into an intimate relationship with Himself. Then He could be an example to them by doing just what He wanted to equip them to do.

71

Jesus wanted to imprint Himself indelibly upon the Twelve. They must imbibe His spirit, share His passion for lost men, and long for His Father's will to be done on earth as in heaven. He understood the dynamics of intimate association: To be like Him they must be near Him, feel His compassion, sense the depths of His love, and experience His grace. Being with the teacher results in becoming like Him. Being in His presence progressively transforms us into His likeness (2 Corinthians 3:18). Being with Jesus, then, does more than produce people who know the mechanics of disciple-making (as we shall see); it produces a burden, a commitment to His cause, and a desire to see His will accomplished.

5 Circle the letter in front of each TRUE completion. According to the foregoing content, Jesus chose the Twelve
a because He knew that it was impossible to train large numbers of people effectively.
b in order to develop a hierarchy of leaders in the church and thus establish effective church government.
c to make disciples of them and equip them for service.
d to develop a succession of leadership that would be centralized in the birthplace of Christianity.
e to prepare them to make disciples of others.

6 Circle the letter in front of each correct response. According to our discussion, *being with Jesus* was important for which of the following reasons?
a) Jesus knew that complete persons would be like their teacher.
b) Jesus knew that a fully-trained person would develop the tendency to think independently without regard for other disciples.
c) Jesus knew that to be fully trained, people must have long and consistent exposure to formal, classroom education, rigid discipline, and a long period of apprenticeship.
d) Jesus knew that *being with a teacher* resulted in the disciple becoming like his teacher.
e) Jesus knew that an intimate relationship produces likeness between a disciple and his teacher.

Teaching Them

Objective 4. *Identify methods Jesus used to teach the Twelve.*

Jesus' involvement with the Twelve, while it can be considered correctly as a teaching-learning relationship, was not a typical school or classroom situation. A typical one-hour class setting would have been insufficient. Jesus and the Twelve lived together. They shared life's experiences. They interacted on the lessons the Master taught and reacted continuously to life situations which demanded the application of their knowledge skills.

Sometimes Jesus taught and the Twelve listened as He introduced and explained truth. They asked questions, seeking clarification concerning His teaching, and He responded gladly to their inquiries. In this enviroment of trust, Jesus fostered a spirit of openness. And in the course of time these twelve men developed a willingness to expose themselves to Him and to each other.

On many occasions the Twelve observed Jesus as He dealt with people and responded to a variety of situations. Often they imitated what they saw Him do. Frequently, however, His words and actions amazed them and they wondered at the wisdom, grace, and power He demonstrated (see, for example, Mark 4:35-41; John 8:1-11). These occasions that seemed incomprehensible made an indelible impression on the Twelve and they pondered them long after their Teacher was gone. On some occasions Jesus deliberately included them in His actions, and thus they learned through practice.

The relationship which the Twelve had with Jesus involved responsibility. In accepting His call, the Twelve acknowledged His leadership role and committed themselves to obey Him. It was mutually understood that they were under His authority. Initially, the degree to which they were committed to Him was questionable; however, following the Resurrection and the Day of Pentecost, none could doubt their total obedience to Him. His challenge became their battle cry—a battle cry that still inspires contemporary disciples of Christ (Matthew 28:19-20).

Jesus taught the Twelve and they learned; however, His teaching was different from what many practice. It involved interpersonal relationships and interaction within their restricted group, as well as with people in a wide variety of real life experiences. Jesus was the example which they sought to imitate. His purpose was to equip them for ministry by making them whole. They must be alert to the issues that concerned all people: equity, social justice, civic responsibility, poverty, loneliness, sorrow, fear, and death. They must see, as He saw, the extent of human need (Matthew 9:35-38). Their field was not limited to religious matters; it was as broad as the needs of the world (Matthew 13:38).

In some respects Jesus' instruction of the Twelve was similar to classroom teaching. For example, the Sermon on the Mount resembled a well-illustrated lecture. At other times He initiated questions that provoked discussion, such as a classroom instructor might (Matthew 16:13). He made use of proven instructional methods and techniques. In other respects His approach was informal and life-oriented (see Matthew 19:13-15 and 16-26). Yet it must be recognized that the approaches Jesus used were appropriate for His goal: to make disciples, to nurture wholeness.

7 Circle the letter in front of the statement which does NOT give one of the methods Jesus used to teach the Twelve. Jesus taught the Twelve
a) by example and through shared life experiences.
b) by requiring them to apply the truth they had learned and by implicitly obeying His directives.
c) as He answered their questions and explained truth more fully to them.
d) primarily through formal classroom interaction.

Commissioning Them

Objective 5. *Select a statement which explains correctly why disciple-making is accepted as the divine method for nurturing spiritual growth.*

Not only did Jesus select the disciple-making for His own ministry but He also commanded Christians to make disciples. Read Matthew 28:18-20 and observe the central feature of the resurrected Christ's challenge to His disciples: *"Go . . . make* disciples . . . *baptizing* them . . . and *teaching* them."* The initiative lay with His followers: they were to go. The nature and extent of their mission was clear: *making disciples of all nations.* The method involved *baptizing* and *teaching.* It is expected that Christians will go to share their faith. As they go, what are they expected to do? The answer is "make disciples." Thus, our Lord passed His method of disciple-making along as the model after which His followers were to pattern their efforts. The following discussion indicated what is involved in performing this one central task.

Jesus gave this commission to make disciples shortly before He returned to heaven. By it He committed to His disciples the responsibility to carry on the ministry He began. In making this commission, Jesus included both the task to be done and the method by which it should be done. He made disciples of the Twelve and then commanded them to go to all nations to make disciples. He sent them out to repeat what He had done to them.

Since this *Great Commission* is the final teaching of Jesus to His disciples before He went back to heaven, we may conclude that disciple-making is the divinely intended method for helping people grow toward Christlikeness. Christian nurture involves making disciples.

8 Match the specific aspect of the commission (right) with the appropriate activity it was meant to generate (left).

....**a** The method by which disciple-making is to be accomplished

....**b** The work of believers in the world

....**c** The initiative for disciple-making

....**d** The extent of believers' work and witness

1) Go
2) Make disciples of all nations
3) Baptizing-teaching

9 Circle the letter in front of the statement which completes correctly this sentence: Disciple-making is accepted as the divine method for Christian nurture because
a) it is logical and easy to accomplish.
b) the Twelve knew that it was the most natural way to gain a following.
c) it was the method commanded by Jesus.
d) it was a familiar system which all Jews understood, acknowledged, and supported.

SOME DIVINE RESOURCES

The Bible reveals that God has given some divine resources to help accomplish the task of nurturing Christian growth. In this section you will consider three important divine resources: 1) the nature of the church, 2) the ministry gifts, and 3) the ministry of the Holy Spirit.

The Nature of the Church

Objective 6. *Recognize statements which explain the nurturing nature of the church.*

Jesus began to build His church during His earthly ministry (Matthew 16:18). The church includes all Christians: those who join themselves to Jesus, seek to grow to maturity in Him, and give expression to the germ of spiritual life He has given them (1 Corinthians 1:1-2).

The church is a living organism. This fact is seen in the Scriptures by the often-used comparison to a body. With this in mind, read carefully Romans 12:1-8, 1 Corinthians 12:12-27, and Ephesians 4:11-16, observing what we can learn about the nature of the church from the illustration of the body.

A body is made up of many different parts. Each part has a particular function to perform. Every part is important because no other member can perform the function of another. The members are interdependent upon each other. If one part of the body fails to develop properly, the whole body is affected adversely. The body cannot be whole and function as it should unless every member functions as it was designed to operate. Because of the interdependence of the various parts of the body, the strength of the whole body comes to the aid of an underdeveloped or sickly part.

You may know of someone who has been badly burned or wounded in some other way. Without proper care the injury can quickly become infected. The result may be that the person becomes very sick. At this point the whole body comes to assist the wounded member, initiating the process of healing. For the healing process is the concern of the whole body. Therefore, after a person has successfully overcome a serious infection, his whole body, not just the affected part, is weakened and needs rest. This is true because the strength and resources of the whole body come to the rescue of the weakened part.

In the body of Christ—the church—the strength and resources of all the members become a resource to help underdeveloped or weakened members achieve health, wholeness, and maturity. Weaker or less mature members can draw strength from stronger, more mature members of the body.

The nature of the church—an organism of interdependent parts, which mutually strengthen the body—is a valuable resource in helping people grow toward spiritual maturity. The fact that the church is a loving, caring, sympathetic organism composed of people who love, care, and give sympathy is a valuable asset in nurturing spiritual growth. Properly, Christian nurture is a ministry of the church which seeks to lead converts into active, meaningful relationships within the local church, the expression of the body of Christ in a given place.

10 In the following exercise match the Scripture reference (right) with the appropriate church or body concept given (left). Some concepts may have more than one Scripture reference.

....**a** The exercise of one's gift is limited only by the degree of his faith and the needs of the body.

....**b** The gifts or ministries in the body of Christ were given to prepare God's people for service, unity of faith, knowledge of spiritual things, and spiritual maturity.

....**c** The body of Christ is made up of interdependent parts, each of which is important to the function of the body.

....**d** The fact that one has and exercises spiritual gifts calls for humble thanks, not pride of possession.

....**e** Body ministries produce spiritual stature and discrimination, plus knowledge of body needs and how to help meet them.

....**f** The body of Christ is a sympathetic unit; therefore, what concerns or affects one member affects the whole body.

....**g** God has appointed various ministries for the church.

1) Romans 12:1-8
2) 1 Corinthians 12:12-27
3) Ephesians 4:11-16

11 Circle the letter in front of each TRUE statement.

a The church is a living organism composed of many interdependent parts.

b In the church each member is expected to mature and function independently of all other members.

c In the church stronger, more mature members are a resource from which weaker, less mature members can draw understanding, care, and strength.

d If any part of the body of Christ fails to develop properly, the whole body will suffer.

e The goal of Christian nurture is to develop the individual; it is not concerned with his relationship to the local church.

The Ministry Gifts

Objective 7. *Choose statements which explain correctly how the ministry gifts nurture spiritual growth and what is one's responsibility in exercising his gift.*

God has given each believer a gift (or some gifts) to equip him for spiritual ministry in the body of Christ. Four biblical passages teach that Christians have received such enablement for ministry: Romans 12:1-8; 1 Corinthians 12; Ephesians 4:11-16; and 1 Peter 4:10-11.

You should study these Scriptures carefully. They contain a whole philosophy of ministry. The following statements form a summary of the important truth they teach:

1. Every believer receives one or more of the ministry gifts.
2. These gifts are given by the Holy Spirit.
3. Not everyone receives the same gift nor should he seek to exercise the same ministry.
4. The body needs the proper exercise of all the gifts.
5. The gifts are equipment for effective Christian service.
6. Proper exercise of the gifts results in the upbuilding of the body.

7. Individual believers are interdependent members of the body; therefore, they have a responsibility to all the other members of the body.

8. The gifts are to be exercised in the spirit of Christian love.

Proper exercise of the various ministry gifts results in the upbuilding of the whole body. In this way the ministry gifts help the spiritual growth of the different members. The church is a mutually ministering body. Each gift contributes to the upbuilding of others. These ministry gifts are resources for the nurturing and upbuilding of Christian life. In this broad, general way the minsitry gifts nurture spiritual growth.

Specifically, it should be observed that teachers are God's special gifts to the church. God has placed them uniquely in the church to nurture the spiritual life of others. Teachers bear special responsibility to help other Christians grow toward wholeness in Christlikeness.

12 Circle the letter in front of each TRUE statement which explains correctly how the ministry gifts nurture spiritual growth.

a The purpose of the ministry gifts is to enable some parts of the body of Christ to function for the benefit of the rest.

b The ministry gifts serve to upbuild the body of Christ.

c Since each believer has some ministry gift, he can minister to others and help them grow spiritually.

d God put teachers in the church to form a unique class of people which has special authority to teach the Bible.

e God put teachers in the church to nurture the spiritual growth of others by teaching God's Word to them.

13 According to the Scripture references and discussion in this section, each believer has what responsibility concerning the exercise of his gift? Each believer

a) may use or refrain from using his gift as he pleases.

b) is challenged to exercise his gift for the common good.

c) must judge whether or not his gift is worthy of use as compared to the gifts of others.

The Ministry of the Holy Spirit

Objective 8. *Identify specific ministries of the Holy Spirit and explain how the Holy Spirit nurtures spiritual growth.*

When Jesus gave His command to "make disciples of all nations," He promised His presence and power as enablement to accomplish this task. This order and the matter of the Holy Spirit's relation to the Twelve were given to the disciples shortly before the Crucifixion. As charter members of the early church, the Twelve were representative of all those who would subsequently respond to the gospel. And what the Spirit's relation was to them He will be to us also.

All newborn Christians need spiritual food (instruction) to grow. We lack spiritual understanding, spiritual appetite, and the incentive to learn spiritual truth. But we have the Holy Spirit, the Counselor and faithful Teacher, who stands ready to supply each of these and many other needs.

You discovered in Lesson 1 that the Word of God is the foundation of Christian nurture. The Scriptures, which reveal God's nature, plan, and will for man, are quickened by God. Second Timothy 3:16-17 and 2 Peter 1:20-21 disclose the Holy Spirit's role in superintending the process of Scripture writing. First, the Spirit revealed the mind of God to the men He chose to record His truth (1 Corinthians 2:10-15). This *revelation* disclosed things to them they could not have known otherwise. As they wrote, the Holy Spirit guided and helped them, inspiring them to write exactly what God wanted them to write. While He employed their vocabularies, learning, and experience in the process, what they wrote was God's Word, not their own. This enablement is referred to as *inspiration* and means literally "God-breathed." Thus, God revealed His whole plan to us by His Spirit, and this we have in the sacred Scriptures.

In a sense, though, we share in this revelatory process, because the Holy Spirit *illuminates* and explains these truths to our hearts also. However, He does not come to reveal new truth to us, for God's truth has been revealed finally, personally, and objectively in Christ.

81

Experience shows that an outward revelation of truth is inadequate, because our knowledge always precedes our application of the truth. We just don't do by nature the things required to grow spiritually (Romans 7). But the Holy Spirit, who is the Teacher, carries on the ministry of Jesus as His representative on earth. And just as He illuminated the minds of the disciples and reminded them of the truth Christ taught them, so the Holy Spirit *illuminates* the truth of the Scriptures to us. He brings new understanding, new comprehension, new illumination; however, He does more than show us the truth; He brings us into the truth, helping us put it into action, making it real and truly significant in our lives. In this way Christ dwells within us and we carry on Christ's work in a way that glorifies Him. Thus, the Holy Spirit *instructs* us through the Word which He inspired His servants to write and nurtures us toward Christlikeness.

Moreover, the Spirit teaches us by inward *illumination*. He speaks to our hearts by His own personal influence and He prompts us at certain times to do certain things. Sometimes He checks us from doing others. On occasion He convicts us when we have said or done something that is not consistent with true Christian character.

He teaches us in response to our sincere hunger for truth as we pray. He is the inerrant, the incomparable Teacher.

Significantly, the Holy Spirit uses us to help others grow as we fill the office of teacher (Ephesians 4:11-12). As you teach God's Word, the Holy Spirit will enable you to understand this truth. Since He is present in every teaching-learning situation, you can be confident that He will help you communicate God's truth effectively. Then those you teach will receive the truth which nurtures spiritual growth. His divine energy strengthens and supports both those who teach and those who receive spiritual truth.

Christian nurture is unique because of the Holy Spirit's ministry:

1. He caused God's Word to be written.
2. He helps us understand God's truth.
3. He empowers and enables us to communicate God's truth.
4. He helps us apply truth to our daily lives.
5. He prompts, influences, and convicts or reproves us.

The Holy Spirit is present to help both the teacher and the learner. The result is that Christians are nurtured, equipped, and empowered to grow toward Christlikeness.

14 Read each of the following Scripture references concerning the ministry of the Holy Spirit and respond to the question associated with each.

a Matthew 28:18-20 and Luke 24:49. What promises are given in these verses? ....

....

b Acts 1:4, 5, 8. What command is given and why?

....

....

c John 14:15-18, 26; 15:26. In His absence Jesus promised to send the .... to be with His followers forever, the .... The Holy Spirit was to be sent in Christ's name to .... the disciples all things and to .... them of the things Christ has said to them. He was to .... about Jesus.

d John 16:13-15. List the things Jesus said the Holy Spirit would accomplish when He came. ....

....

e 1 Corinthians 2:5-15. What does the Spirit do in this instance and why? ....

....

15 Match the specific ministry of the Holy Spirit (right) with its appropriate description (left).

....**a** Activity in which the Holy Spirit corrects one for doing or saying something inconsistent with Christian conduct

....**b** Activity by which one is borne along by the Spirit so that He says what God wants said

....**c** The act through which the Spirit discloses the mind, will, or purposes of God which could not otherwise be known

....**d** Activity by which the Spirit enlightens believers concerning the work of Christ and prompts and directs their lives progressively toward Christlikeness

....**e** Activity of the Spirit by which one learns what God has in store for him

1) Revelation
2) Inspiration
3) Illumination
4) Conviction or reproof

16 In your notebook, explain briefly how the Holy Spirit nurtures spiritual growth.

PATTERNS OF NURTURING SPIRITUAL GROWTH

Objective 9. *Choose statements which differentiate between informal and formal patterns of Christian nurture.*

The church collectively and believers individually are challenged to nurture spiritual life, helping people develop toward Christlikeness. In many churches this task of nurturing has been centralized in a Christian education program or department. Other churches have tended to view this ministry of disciple-making a bit differently, believing that nurturing arises out of the regular ministries of the church and the informal associations provided by the church. While approaches to Christian nurture differ, the fact remains that Christian nurture requires both formal and informal methods.

Regardless of the approach, God's Word is the spiritual food which nurtures spiritual growth. Intimate, caring Christian relationships also promote spiritual growth. Communicating the truth of God's Word is often done by more traditional, formal approaches to teaching-learning. Relational teaching is accomplished through more informal techniques, in which a more mature Christian associates with less mature Christians and becomes an example to them, demonstrating how to live the Christian life effectively. The less mature Christian learns by identification and imitation. We, then, can say that the ministry of nurturing spiritual growth requires both informal and formal patterns.

Informal patterns involve nurturing spiritual growth through activities other than traditional schooling methods. The relationships Jesus established with the Twelve, the way He approached the task of making disciples of them, is an excellent example of the informal pattern of Christian nurture.

The relationships which exist in the body of Christ, the exercise of the mutuality of ministry as each uses his ministry gift for the development and welfare of all other members, clearly show that the church is equipped for the relational teaching that is characteristic of informal patterns of Christian nurture.

Formal patterns of nurturing Christian growth are intended more for communicating facts and information. Learning Bible content, doctrinal information, and material that can be classified as knowledge can be taught well through formal patterns. Formal patterns closely resemble schooling. In the process of making disciples Jesus sometimes used traditional, formal patterns of teaching information. He did not use a schoolroom as the setting, but He did make use of the approach and is considered to have been masterful in its use. While the goal of Christian nurture is not a head filled with facts and knowledge but a life lived with Christ as the center, some factual information must be learned. Classes, seminars, and similar activities are excellent means of transmitting knowledge to less mature Christians. This knowledge becomes an agent of change, enabling Christians to increase in spiritual stature and become more Christlike.

Effective Christian nurture will include both informal and formal patterns. If you are helping another Christian grow spiritually, you will want to build an intimate relationship with him. You will want to model the Christ life in such a way that he can see an example of how it is meant to be lived by watching you. You will also want to help this person understand biblical and doctrinal truth. You may find yourself teaching classes in the formal tradition of education. Christian nurture involves both informal and formal patterns. Neither alone is sufficient. If you are helping Christians grow spiritually, you will need to make use of both patterns.

17 Distinguish between formal and informal patterns of nurturing spiritual growth, placing a 1) in front of formal examples and a 2) in front of those that are examples of informal patterns.

....**a** Jesus' method of nurturing spiritual growth was accomplished by being with the Twelve.

....**b** Paul admonished Timothy to be an example or model of Christian life.

....**c** Pastor Berg gives a series of studies to those who are seeking to become more mature. Students have assignments and are expected to be able to discuss the lesson content in class.

....**d** Pastor Devon has his congregation organized into small groups for monthly meetings, where they can have fellowship, pray, or study as they feel led.

....**e** Paul states that he was thoroughly trained in the Law under Gamaliel.

self-test

1 The biblical concept of disciple-making is related to growth and development in
a) an indirect way, since one is of primary and the other of secondary importance.
b) no way: one can only make disciples out of the spiritually mature.
c) the sense only that both are spiritual matters.
d) a direct way, for as one becomes a disciple and develops spiritually he becomes like his Master.

2 Disciple-making is similar to the process by which an apprentice becomes a master because (according to this lesson)
a) a disciple acquires the skills of his teacher by imitating his teacher's theories and ideas.
b) the disciple learns by conforming to the likeness of his teacher, growing spiritually in the process.
c) a disciple cannot be effective until he has served for years as an assistant.
d) the disciple must select only the best teacher if he is ever to become a mature teacher himself.

3 The purpose or goal of disciple-making, according to our discussion, is to help people mature spiritually, that is, to grow toward

a) spiritual self-sufficiency.   c) Christlikeness.

b) adequacy in social life.   d) the apostolic model.

4 Jesus nurtured spiritual growth, according to Mark's Gospel, by having the Twelve *with Him* and then *sending them out* so that they would be

a) equipped for service and seasoned in the application of disciple-making principles.

b) near enough to correct them when they made mistakes and yet able to develop according to their own desires.

c) under His influence and thus incapable of thinking or acting on their own.

d) tutored adequately in both theory and practice and thus able to conform to current educational practice.

5 The *nature of the church*, we have learned, is a significant resource in nurturing spiritual growth because

a) only institutional strength and resources can meet the vast amount of human need.

b) its organizational structure is necessary to dispense the specific growth materials needed by individual believers.

c) the church is an organism of interdependent parts which lends body support, strength, and health to each part.

d) the church collectively has been given the assignment of nurturing spiritual growth, not individual members.

6 Ministry gifts nurture spiritual growth as

a) a broad range of believers exercising various gifts is able to minister effectively to the growth needs of developing believers.

b) a few members of the body of Christ exercise gifts for the benefit of many developing members who don't possess gifts.

c) some select believers develop stature and status in the body of Christ, exercising their gifts from time to time.

d) one responds to the prompting of the Holy Spirit: if he responds, he is rewarded by spiritual growth; if he doesn't he won't merit such growth.

7 The Holy Spirit nurtures spiritual growth in all of the following ways but one. Which statement does NOT represent one of these ways?
a) He gave us God's Word and helps us understand it.
b) He moves us, often against our will, to conform to the likeness of Christ.
c) He helps us communicate God's truth and apply it to our daily lives also.
d) He prompts us, convicts, and influences us in the course of our daily lives.

8 The *formal patterns* of nurturing Christian growth are characterized by
a) little or no structure and a one-to-one student/teacher relationship.
b) rigid structure and very little flexibility in approaching the teacher-learning situation.
c) the use of traditional educational methods which are often associated with classroom situations.
d) the association of teacher and learner on a relational basis.

9 The informal patterns of nurturing Christian growth are characterized by
a) a loose or careless approach to the learning situation with a disregard for formal, traditional learning methods.
b) the casual approach people employ in transmitting knowledge.
c) reliance on example apart from learning factual information, which may contaminate pure character.
d) personal associations and relationships, modeling or identification, and activities.

10 Of formal and informal patterns of nurturing Christian growth we can say most accurately, based on the lesson content, that
a) formal patterns work best for mature Christians while informal patterns are best for less mature Christians.
b) effective Christian nurture will include both patterns, for each has an important function in the growth process.
c) traditionally, formal patterns have been used exclusively; however, today the informal approach is considered best.
d) large, organized groups use formal patterns to the best advantage; whereas, smaller ones find the informal approach best.

Before you continue your study with Lesson 4, be sure to complete your unit student report for Unit 1 and return the answer sheet to your ICI instructor.

answers to study questions

9 c) it was the method commanded by Jesus.

1 a False.
  b True.
  c False.
  d True.

10 a 1) Romans 12:1-8.
  b 3) Ephesians 4:11-16.
  c 2) 1 Corinthians 12:12-27.
  d 1) Romans 12:1-8.
  e 3) Ephesians 4:11-16.
  f 2) 1 Corinthians 12:12-27.
  g 1) Romans 12:1-8   and 3) Ephesians 4:11-16.

2 b) in that the disciple learns by observing, being with, and doing the teacher's bidding.

11 a True.
  b False.
  c True.
  d True.
  e False.

3 a True.
  b False.
  c False.
  d True.

12 a False.
  b True.
  c True.
  d False.
  e True.

4 c) that of appealing to many for commitment.

13 b) is challenged to exercise his gift for the common good.

5 a False.
  b False.
  c True.
  d False.
  e True.

14 a That He would be with them always and that He would send what the Father promised to clothe them with, heavenly power.
  b They were to stay in Jerusalem until they received the Father's promised gift, the Holy Spirit. The Holy Spirit's coming on them would enable them to become Christ's worldwide witnesses.
  c Counselor, Spirit of Truth, teach, remind, testify.
  d You should have noted the following: He would guide His followers into all truth, not speak on His own, speak only what He hears (that is, He would faithfully represent Jesus), reveal future events, and glorify Jesus by teaching Jesus' followers His words.
  e He searches the things of God. This He does so that He may reveal to us what God has provided for us. His teaching gives us spiritual discernment and helps us mature spiritually.

6 a) Jesus knew that complete persons would be like their teacher.
  d) Jesus knew that *being with a teacher* resulted in the disciple becoming like his teacher.
  e) Jesus knew that an intimate relationship produces likeness between a disciple and his teacher.

15 a 4) Conviction or reproof.
  b 2) Inspiration.
  c 1) Revelation.
  d 3) Illumination.
  e 1) Revelation and 3) Illumination. (The Spirit discloses the Word of God and in so doing the believer is illuminated or enlightened.)

7 d) primarily through formal classroom interaction.

16 Your answer may differ a bit from mine. I've noted that initially the Holy Spirit was the agent of revelation, communicating God's truth to man. Since Christ's first coming, He serves as the Counselor, the ambassador, of our Lord to all believers. He illuminates Christ's words to our hearts. He quickens us to receive enlightenment from God's Word, reproves us when we do or say things inappropriate to Christian conduct, checks us when a course of action may be harmful, teaches us, and influences us for good. In addition, He enables us to teach others, giving us both divine wisdom and insight into the truth so that we can help them grow and mature spiritually.

8 a 3) Baptizing-teaching.
  b 2) Make disciples of all nations.
  c 1) Go.
  d 2) Make disciples of all nations.

17 a 2) Informal.
  b 2) Informal.
  c 1) Formal.
  d 2) Informal.
  e 1) Formal.

Unit 2

GROWING AND LEARNING

LESSON 4

Discovering and Doing

Juan was pleased when Maria was given the bread recipe which had been used by her mother and grandmother for years. He had always enjoyed the warm, crusty loaves that the women in her family baked. Maria read the recipe then placed it on the kitchen table. She proceeded to make her bread dough using the same ingredients and recipe she had used since she and Juan had married. After only one bite of the freshly baked bread, Juan knew Maria's bread was not like her mother's. Maria had all the instructions for baking delicious bread, but she had continued in her old method of making dough without making any changes in her recipe. Without making the changes the new recipe called for, there was no way Maria's bread could taste like her mother's!

You may recall some experience in which you learned new information but did not act on it at once. Learning includes discovering truth, but it does not end there. Learning should also lead one to apply the truth he has learned to his daily life experiences. In this lesson you will study how people learn and discover that learning involves discovering truth and acting on that truth in making appropriate changes in behavior.

lesson outline

Two Concepts of Learning
Changing the Learner
Levels of Learning
How People Learn
Learning to Nurture Christian Growth

lesson objectives

When you finish this lesson you should be able to:

■ Recognize that learning must involve personal interaction with and application of the lesson to life situations if appropriate changes are to be made in one's knowledge, attitudes, and behavior.

■ Describe how people learn by identifying various levels of learning ranging from simple to complex involvement with lesson material.

■ Discuss how those involved in Christian nurture may facilitate the learning and internalizing of spiritual truth so that learners may become more Christlike in their thinking, attitudes, and actions.

learning activities

1. Study the lesson and answer the study questions in the usual manner.

2. Learn the meanings of any key words that are new to you.

3. Take the self-test at the end of the lesson and check your answers.

key words

acquisition	generalizations	relevant
assimilate	necessitates	retention
conditioning	permeates	verbatim
convictions	perpetuate	

lesson development

TWO CONCEPTS OF LEARNING

Objective 1. *Evaluate and correctly classify activities to determine whether they result in transfer or discovery learning.*

You already have some understanding of what *learning* and *teaching* are, no doubt. Your definitions may not be technical nor formalized, but you have some idea what these words mean.

1 Write a simple definition of these terms as you presently understand them.

a Learning is ...... *GAINING IN KNOWLEDGE + SKILL*

b Teaching is ...... *INPARTING THE ABOVE*

You were asked to write a definition of these terms as you understand them. Since you wrote what you think, there can be no right or wrong answers. Many people hold either one or the other of two popular points of view on this matter. As I explain them, you decide which view is more like the one you wrote.

Some people regard telling as teaching and listening as learning. If someone tells a story, states facts, or explains information, it is assumed he has taught. And if someone listens when a teacher does these things, it is assumed that he has learned. The learner may be expected to write or copy the teacher's words and memorize them. If the learner can recall the information later and recite the teacher's exact words, according to this view, he has demonstrated mastery of the material—he has learned.

Teachers who perceive the teaching-learning process in this way talk a lot and require their learners to sit and quietly listen. They believe that *teachers teach lessons*; therefore, they view the lesson content as the key element in the process. To them, teaching is seen as the transfer of information from the teacher to the learner. How do you suppose this interpretation affects the teacher's performance in the classroom?

The teacher, in this context, is considered a source of knowledge. He is supposed to have extensive knowledge of the subject, and the learner is viewed as having little or no knowledge of the subject. The teacher's task, therefore, is to transfer his superior knowledge of the subject to the "empty mind" of the learner. This concept of the teaching-learning process has led many teachers to attempt to lecture rapidly in order to cover many facts, complete their lessons, and give the learner maximum exposure to much information. Because this view expects a transfer of knowledge from the teacher to the learner, it is called the *transfer approach* or *transfer learning*.

Another method of teaching operates on the assumption that the learner is the subject of the operation and must be involved in the process. Adherents of this point of view believe that the learner should be equipped to do more than merely recite the information correctly. They want the learner to understand the material and be able to relate it to previous knowledge, developing some personal convictions about it and learning to use it in establishing values as a basis for solving life's problems. This approach requires the learner to interact personally with the material; the learner must discover truth through his own efforts.

Notice the different emphasis in this second approach: the teacher teaches a person rather than a lesson. The learner and the results of his learning are the important elements. This teaching method requires the teacher to guide the learner in the process of learning. Its adherents do not equate *filling the learner's mind with knowledge* with significant learning; they do believe that the teacher can and should help the learner discover and apply truth. Because of this, this view is called the *discovery approach* or *discovery learning*.

The "transfer approach" seeks to fill the learner with information.

The "discovery approach" seeks to lead the learner to discover truth for himself.

2 Read the two stories which follow. Then write 1) in front of each question that is an example of *transfer learning* and 2) if it is an example of *discovery learning*.

 Brigette has taught a children's Bible study class each Sunday at her church for several months. "Okay, girls and boys, please sit down now. Fold your hands and sit quietly while I teach you the Bible lesson," she says regularly as she begins her lesson. She then proceeds to tell a Bible story while the children sit and listen to her.

Pierre, also, has been teaching a children's Bible class at another church for some time. If you were to look in on his class, you would find the learners moving about the room busily engaged in making props for the Bible story they have been discussing. Or you might find each one restating in turn an aspect of the Bible lesson to the group and telling what one can learn from the biblical example. Or again, they may be seen acting out the story. No matter when you looked in, you would see them involved in various activities and freely talking about the Bible story.

....**a** Based on her performance in the classroom, Brigette appears to be influenced by which approach to teaching and learning?

....**b** The description of Pierre's classroom in session demonstrates that he has adopted which approach to teaching and learning?

....**c** Which approach is more like the definition you wrote for question **1**?

3 In which one of the above-mentioned classes would you expect to find more learning taking place—learning that builds on the basis of previous knowledge and experience and prepares the learner to find solutions to problems? Why? Write your answers in your notebook.

Brigette holds more to the transfer view, doesn't she? When she is teaching, telling the Bible story, she believes the children are learning while they listen, and they are to some degree. Pierre, however, uses the discovery approach. He wants the learners to interact personally with the material, and he has arranged different activities to help them make discoveries for themselves.

You may have attended classes where both of these concepts of teaching and learning were followed. In the past, the transfer approach was common, and it is still used; however, modern teachers tend to follow the discovery approach. The discovery approach is based on current understanding which has resulted from psychological and educational research. If you have studied under the transfer approach, you may have wondered if it was the best

101

approach. It is indeed important to understand many facts that concern us in today's world. And it is important to be able to remember and recall this information which helps us to be knowledgeable and alert to life around us. However, it is far more practical to understand the facts you have learned in a way which can be applied to the actual solving of real life problems. The ability to apply knowledge, as we shall see, comes through experience, through use.

Please memorize the following definitions of *teaching* and *learning*. You will be required to recognize the correct definitions of these words in the self-test and in the student report.

1. Learning is discovering information and making desired responses to that information.
2. Teaching is helping people learn.

Perhaps you are beginning to understand that teaching and learning are interdependent. Generally speaking, if one teaches effectively, according to the foregoing definition, learning results. If receptive learners fail to learn anything, effective teaching has not taken place. We may think of teaching and learning as two sides of one coin. They are inseparably joined as two parts of one whole concept. Because of this, we will refer to the process as *teaching-learning*.

4 Write 1) in front of each activity below that results in *transfer learning* and 2) if it results in *discovery learning*.

....**a** Memorizing Bible verses

....**b** Discussing alternative viewpoints

....**c** Researching a concept

....**d** Listening to a lecture

....**e** Doing an experiment

....**f** Copying information from a chalkboard

....**g** Locating a city on a map

....**h** Hearing a story

CHANGING THE LEARNER

Objective 2. *Identify learning results associated with change through a learning type.*

Change is essential to learning. The learner discovers information and responds to it. If the learner does not change, learning has not taken place; and if learning has not taken place, teaching has been ineffective.

5 Read Matthew 28:19-20 and observe particularly Jesus' command. Write on the line below what disciples are to be taught to do.

....

Do you understand the connection between teaching disciples to "obey" everything Jesus commanded and our observation that learners must change if learning occurs? How could someone "obey" the commands of Jesus without first understanding them and then building his life on them? Obedience implies fully accepting and doing what is learned. Knowledge must be translated into action if it is to be effective. The major goal of learning, then, is for the learner to put truth into action, being convinced of truth to the point of making it his own and changing his life accordingly.

Our efforts to nurture Christian growth are particularly affected by this concept. Our goal is to see people changed by helping them grow in Christ so that His life can find living expression through their lives. Christian nurture helps people to be changed progressively into the likeness of Jesus. When we become Christians, our lives may be far from Christlike; however, as His life grows within us and we adjust ourselves to what we learn about Him, we take on His likeness.

6 Based on the foregoing information, circle the letters in front of the statements which complete correctly the following sentence. Learning takes place when
a) teachers do all the talking.
b) learners change consistent with the truth.
c) learners listen carefully but give little indication of any response.
d) learners put truth into action.
e) learners discover and respond to information.
f) learners hear truth and do nothing about it.

Change must occur in learners if learning is to take place. But how are learners expected to change? As a child grows, he changes. He most often continues to look much the same, yet he gradually takes on more adult-like characteristics. Changes are expected with growth. Learning change is generally thought of as growth, maturing, or adjustment.

Educators have identified three areas in which learning changes occur. These areas are: 1) knowledge, 2) attitudes, and 3) behavior. It helps me to remember these by thinking of them as the head (knowledge), the heart (attitudes), and the hands (behavior). All learning change occurs in these three areas.

Change in knowledge may include adding new information, correcting a point of view, or acquiring new or increased support for a viewpoint. Changes in attitudes involve values and feelings. Changed values or feelings may reflect an increased or decreased degree of feeling about something. Changes in behavior often involve the skills that are required to do something. These changes may include developing new skills or becoming better, faster, or more efficient in the performance of a task. Quite frequently in the spiritual realm changes also include a changing of goals and the changing of habits—discontinuing those that are detrimental to Christian growth and acquiring those that encourage it.

The area of attitudes is the most difficult to change. People tend to cling to their values. Human emotions run deep and a change in values necessitates adjustment in emotions and attitudes. Changing values is not easy; nevertheless, this area is a primary concern of those involved in nurturing Christian growth. With proper teaching, however, changes can be brought about in all three areas.

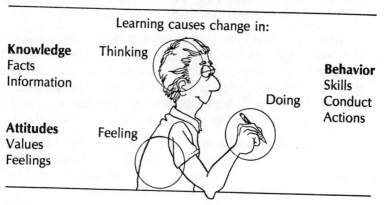

Learning causes change in:

Knowledge
Facts
Information

Thinking

Behavior
Skills
Conduct
Actions

Doing

Attitudes
Values
Feelings

Feeling

7 Match each activity (left) with the appropriate area of change (right).

....**a** Memorizes Bible verses

....**b** Love for God deepens

....**c** Learns to cut out a picture

....**d** Feels sorrow about another's problems

....**e** Changes view on a doctrinal issue

....**f** Learns to direct a Bible study group

....**g** Gains new facts to support a belief already held

....**h** Senses urgency of task more intensely

....**i** Develops technique for effective witnessing

....**j** Acquires skills for teaching a Sunday school class

....**k** Builds a logical argument for God's existence

....**l** Desires to perpetuate church traditions

1) Knowledge
2) Attitude
3) Behavior

LEVELS OF LEARNING

Objective **3**. *From a given list, select the level of learning associated with the activity described.*

When can you say you know someone? Do you know someone after having met him just once? You may know him well enough to recognize him when you see him again and you may remember his name, but do you really know him? Many encounters are required to know someone well. We might say that a growing acquaintance with someone is marked by degrees or levels of friendship.

Similarly, there are various levels of learning. We learn some information at one level and other information at another level. Educators have identified four levels by different terms, and each one is often found where nurturing is taking place.

LEVELS OF LEARNING

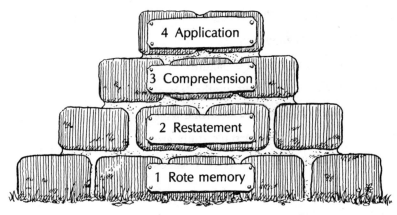

1. *Rote memory*. The learner memorizes facts of information and is able to recall or recognize the information later.

Example: The learner memorizes and recites a Bible verse verbatim.

Not an example: The learner explains a Bible verse using his own words.

106

2. *Restatement.* The learner knows material well-enough to restate it in his own words. He can change information into different forms without changing the meaning.

Example: The learner writes a paraphrase of a Scripture passage or states a doctrinal point in his own words without changing the meaning.

Not an example: The learner writes a statement of doctrine exactly as it appears in the Statement of Fundamental Doctrines.

3. *Comprehension.* The learner discovers relationships among facts, integrates new information into what he has already learned, makes generalizations, forms values, and develops skills.

Example: The learner understands the meaning of a scriptural principle and applies it to his own life.

Not an example: The learner repeats what the teacher said without understanding the terms or their meanings.

4. *Application.* The learner uses information to solve life's problems, modify his attitudes and behavior, and make evaluations of good or bad, right or wrong. As he applies information in new and concrete situations, he engages in original, creative thinking. These abilities require the identification of issues and the selection and use of appropriate data and skills to resolve issues and solve problems.

Example: The learner changes his habits or practices to conform to a scriptural command or principle.

Not an example: The learner hears the biblical teaching about tithing explained but fails to give any of his money in the offering.

8 Indicate the level of learning associated with each of the following activities by writing the number of the level (listed below) on the line in front of each activity.

1) Rote memory   3) Comprehension
2) Restatement   4) Application

....**a** Quoting John 3:16 from memory

....**b** Rewriting Psalm 23, using a contemporary figure instead of the ancient figure of a shepherd

....**c** Combining truth from two passages of Scripture and concluding a principle from them

....**d** Loving an enemy after studying Jesus' teaching in the Sermon on the Mount

....**e** Explaining in his own words the meaning of the word *salvation*

....**f** Identifying the correct completion to a Bible verse after choosing from a list of four possible completions

....**g** Developing a Bible study using information discovered while listening to a sermon

....**h** Understanding the need for spiritual maturity after comparing several Bible verses together

....**i** Comparing a new discovery from the Bible with truth learned previously

....**j** Volunteering to teach a Bible class after discovering the relationship between teaching and spiritual maturity

....**k** Singing a song without the aid of a songbook

....**l** Describing one of the four levels of learning, using his own words

....**m** Giving his own definition of faith without consulting a Bible dictionary

....**n** Stating a textbook answer to a question asked by the teacher

....**o** Concluding that he made a wrong choice in a troublesome area of his life after studying a lesson from the life of Joseph

....**p** Sensing he should change his behavior after discovering a biblical concept

HOW PEOPLE LEARN

Objective 4. *Relate the ways people learn with various teaching-learning activities.*

It is an accepted fact that people learn. What factors are involved in human learning? How do people learn?

Through the Senses

The five senses—seeing, hearing, smelling, touching, and tasting—are doorways through which people physically experience their environment. People learn more through some senses than through others. Educational research indicates that people learn through the senses in approximately the following proportions:

HOW WE LEARN

Seeing 83%
Hearing 11%
Smelling 3.5%
Touching 1.5%
Tasting 1%

Seeing and hearing are considered the two most effective senses for learning. Learning is greatly increased when information is both seen and heard. And retention is considerably greater when information is perceived by more than one of the senses.

WHAT WE RETAIN

10% .... of what we READ
20% .... of what we HEAR
30% .... of what we SEE
50% .... of what we SEE and HEAR
70% .... of what we HEAR and TELL
90% .... of what we HEAR and DO

Therefore, to facilitate learning and increase retention, learning activities should involve more than one of the senses. Ideally, the learning experience is maximized when the learner responds either verbally to what he has heard or actively by doing something in response to what he has heard.

Compare mentally what you have learned earlier in this lesson about the need for the learner to obey the truth and what you have discovered here about the senses. Learning through hearing and doing is retained longest. Using truth as the basis for making life choices and guiding actions is the goal of learning.

Through Involvement

The learner alone can do the learning. He must discover truth for himself through personal interaction with the information. No one else can learn for him or force him to learn. The learner must personally interact with the material for desired changes to occur. This involvement may be *intellectual*, *emotional*, or *physical*, and in Christian nurture we may add *spiritual* involvement. People learn through a direct, active involvement and interaction with the material.

While we cannot learn for another nor force him to learn, we can plan learning activities which provide opportunities that facilitate learner interaction with the truth. If you are helping someone grow spiritually, you can create a setting for the lesson, provide resources, and structure experiences which will lead him to discover, change, and learn.

Through Practice

People learn by practice or conditioning. When an action is repeated many times it usually becomes a habit. After that, quite routinely, without planning or even thinking about the activity, we continue to perform in the same way we have practiced. Talking is learned in this way. We learn to ride a bicycle by practice, and we learn to swim by swimming. We develop patterns of behavior in the Christian life, too, such as reading the Bible, praying, attending church, and obeying God's Word.

Conditioning is considered a low level of learning because it does not require understanding by the learner. We develop habits simply by repeating the action frequently. It is quite possible to act habitually without understanding the significance of the action or realizing what is taking place. Both positive and negative factors are involved in the formation of habits. As you teach others and help them mature toward Christlikeness, you must be aware of these factors and use this principle wisely.

Through Problem Solving

Problem solving is a means by which people learn. When faced with a difficult situation, people tend to find a solution. A common saying points up this truth: "Necessity is the mother of invention."

In teaching situations, it may be helpful to begin with problems the teacher and students can solve together. As the learners are led into the Bible and other resources, meaningful solutions are found. The teacher guides the learners through problem solving situations, but he does not provide answers to every problem. As a learner considers possible alternatives and decides on a course of action, learning takes place. In this way his critical thinking skills begin to develop, and the learner begins to solve problems on his own initiative.

9 Match the learning activities (left) with the ways people learn (right) by placing the appropriate numbers on the lines in front of each activity.

.... **a** Locating Bible verses

.... **b** Seeing a picture

.... **c** Making a model of the tabernacle

.... **d** Deciding between two choices

.... **e** Hearing a story

.... **f** Memorizing Scriptures

.... **g** Solving a conflict with a neighbor

.... **h** Doing a workbook assignment

1) Through the senses
2) Through involvement
3) Through practice
4) Through problem solving

Human learning is not simple. Many factors such as the nature of the individual, natural ability, interests and needs, background, and values are involved in the learner discovering truth for himself and applying it in his own life experiences. Learning is equipping for life. Planning activities which lead the learner to interact with truth and structuring learning opportunities which enable him to recognize when and how to apply the lesson material for making choices and solving problems are a major function of the teacher.

LEARNING TO NURTURE CHRISTIAN GROWTH

Objective 5. *Select statements which relate learning and Christian nurture.*

Learning involves discovering and doing—interacting personally with truth and putting that truth into practice in life. The learner must change. He must grow through modifying knowledge, adjusting attitudes, and correcting behavior.

These fundamentals of learning are essential to Christian nurture. Christian nurture is life-centered. It involves more than acquiring biblical and spiritual knowledge. Christian nurture is a process for changing lives into the likeness of Christ, enabling people to grow toward spiritual maturity.

There is a body of revealed spiritual truth to be studied. God has revealed Himself in the form of written truth. Christians involved in the nurturing process will encourage people to study the Scriptures and know this information.

Those involved with Christian nurture also recognize that attitudes and values are of prime importance. Attitudinal changes are basic to the task of Christian nurture. Jesus taught that the very essence of the Christian is to love God with his total being. This love, which is an expression of the will, is extended to his neighbor, and ultimately, it is revealed in his own self-concept. Love permeates the attitudes and values of a Christian, and how these attitudes are projected depends on how one has learned to express them. Growing spiritually and becoming more Christlike helps us make attitude adjustments to be more like Him.

Likewise, knowing and feeling are not enough. Full obedience to Christ is necessary. We are not fulfilling our responsibility to nurture Christian growth until the truth finds living expression in believers. Obedient conduct is basic to the Christian life. Since our task in Christian nurture is to foster spiritual life, we must seek to help people grow until the life of Christ finds mature, living expression in their behavior.

10 Circle the letter in front of each TRUE statement.
a Christian nurture seeks to bring about change primarily through knowledge.
b Learning involves changing knowledge, attitudes, and behavior.
c Since the nurturing ministry seeks change in many areas, few short-term gains result form these efforts.
d Christian nurture involves changing lives to conform to the pattern set by our Lord.
e Christian nurture involves learning biblical truth.

f Since truth is powerful and life-changing, we need not encourage or direct change; all initiative for change should originate with the learner.

g As we nurture Christian growth, our attempt, essentially, is geared to change in the area of knowledge.

h In the process of Christian nurture, learning leads to the life of Christ finding appropriate expression in Christians.

self-test

1 According to this lesson, learning that changes the knowledge, attitudes, and behavior of the learner must involve his interaction with an application of the lesson to life situations because
a) what one sees and hears alone is seldom retained.
b) lessons which require an action response are retained much longer than those which do not require interaction.
c) what one *does* is more important than what one *thinks*.
d) what one *does* is more important than what one *is*.

2 If a Christian is told that it is his responsibility to share the gospel with others, we know he has learned the lesson best if he
a) reads extensively on the subject of stewardship and evangelism.
b) attends many seminars on soul-winning and effective witnessing.
c) receives the message of his duties well and gives whole-hearted approval.
d) takes advantage of an opportunity to share Christ with an unbeliever.

3 Jesus' parable of the house built on the sand by the foolish man (Matthew 7:24-27) represents the unheeding hearer of truth. It teaches us that
a) not all people have the ability to understand truth.
b) change for the good is made in one's life when he applies the truth to life situation.
c) knowledge is more important than action.
d) action is not dependent upon knowledge.

4 Some teachers who employ the *transfer approach* to learning judge the outcome of their efforts on the basis of students' ability to remember the information exactly as it was given. This response calls for what kind of learning?
a) Rote memory   c) Comprehension
b) Restatement   d) Application

5 According to the facts we have studied, the discovery approach to learning emphasizes all of the following except one. Which statement is NOT emphasized by this approach?
a) The learner should be involved in the learning process, understanding new material and relating it to what he already knows.
b) The learner should develop some personal convictions about the material he learns.
c) The lesson content is the key element in the teaching-learning process.
d) The learner should learn to use the material in establishing values as a basis for solving life's problems.

6 Jesus' command to make disciples of all nations, teaching them to obey everything He commanded them implies that
a) the change in learners is evidence that learning has occurred.
b) learning involves accepting truth and applying it to one's life.
c) teaching is comprehended in this: it is giving the learner all the truth.
d) all of the above: a), b), and c).
e) the things mentioned above in a) and b) are correct.

7 All learning change occurs in three areas: knowledge, attitudes, and behavior. The area of attitudes is most difficult to change because
a) of the difficulty one experiences in adding new information to his existing knowledge.
b) people hold tightly to their values and any change requires adjustment in one's emotions and attitudes.
c) it is difficult to learn and apply new skills to one's life situation.
d) it means acquiring new or increased support for a point of view.

8 According to our study, educational research indicates that learning involves
a) primarily one kind or level of learning which simply matures as one learns.
b) learning by degrees all the information one will ever learn in life.
c) various levels of learning: we learn some information at one level and some at other levels.
d) three stages: early, middle, and later periods, during which we assimilate all factual knowledge.

9 The experience of the learner who is at the rote memory learning level is characterized by the ability to
a) memorize facts and recall or recognize them at a later time.
b) know facts sufficiently well so that he is able to express them accurately in his own words.
c) use information to solve problems and engage in creative thinking.
d) discover relationships among facts and integrate new information into the body of knowledge he has already acquired.

10 When a learner is able to use information to solve life's problems, modify his attitudes and behavior, and make appropriate value judgments we say he is at what learning level?
a) Rote memory
b) Application
c) Comprehension
d) Restatement

11 When the learner knows material well enough to change it into different forms without changing the meaning, using his own words, he is operating at which learning level?
a) Comprehension   c) Rote memory
b) Application   d) Restatement

12 The learning level at which the learner discovers relationships among facts, integrates new information with what he already knows, makes generalizations, forms values, and develops skills is
a) Comprehension   c) Rote memory
b) Application   d) Restatement

13 One of the generalizations we can safely make about how people learn is that people learn
a) equally through all their senses.
b) best through a combination of any two of the senses.
c) most effectively through their seeing and hearing senses.
d) regardless of the senses employed in the learning process.

14 Educational research, as we have seen in this lesson, indicates that retention is greatest when
a) more than one of the senses is employed in learning activities.
b) one sees and hears information presented.
c) one hears and tells what he has learned.
d) the learner hears and then acts upon what he has heard.

15 In our discussion of "how people learn," all of the following statements were noted except one. Which one was NOT noted?
a) The learner must personally interact with the material for changes to occur (through involvement).
b) The learner learns by conditioning, by repeating an action until it becomes a habit (through practice).
c) The learner, when faced with a difficult situation, tends to find a solution (through problem solving).
d) The learner performs best and learns most rapidly when he learns on his own without directions or instructions (through self-motivation).

16-17 Consider each of the following examples carefully to see which learning approach is employed and what level of learning is likely to occur. Then discuss briefly the positive or negative factors you see in the approach. You might offer either a suggestion for improvement or a justification for the use of that particular approach.

16 Rolf teaches a large adult Bible class. He stands in front of the class and lectures each Sunday. He has good notes, is well-prepared, and uses many examples and experiences from life to illustrate his lesson content. He uses maps and visual aids, also, to help students learn the facts better. Some students take notes while he talks; most sit quietly listening, giving him their full attention. He expects the learners to "know" the material he has covered. He believes that their performance on a weekly quiz (which calls for recognition of the precise points he has made) demonstrates their mastery of the material. Circle the letter in front of the learning approach he uses and the letter in front of the level of learning likely to occur.

a) Transfer learning d) Restatement
b) Discovery learning e) Comprehension
c) Recognition f) Application

....

....

17 Sheri is the teacher of a Bible class for secondary students. She has the students seated around large tables on which are some concordances, Bible dictionaries, Bible atlases, paper, and pencils (as well as various other miscellaneous Bible reference books). She usually gives a brief overview of the lesson and then writes a number of relevant questions on the chalkboard. While she encourages students to volunteer answers, she watches carefully to see that no one is left out of the discussions as she directs the interaction and projects. Often the students state in their own words what lessons they can learn from their studies, how this knowledge affects the way they think, feel, and behave, and how new information fits into their current value system and knowledge. They are encouraged to use the knowledge gained to solve life problems and to add to their own value system. Sheri tends to evaluate their progress on the basis of their responses, as well as their behavior and attitude changes. Circle the letter in front of the learning approach Sheri uses and that in front of the highest level of learning likely to occur in her class.

a) Transfer learning   d) Restatement
b) Discovery learning   e) Comprehension
c) Recognition   f) Application

....

....

....

18 Teaching, as we learned in this lesson, is defined as
a) telling someone something.
b) directing activities that keep people busy.
c) helping people to learn.
d) convincing someone of the correctness and reasonableness of something.

19 Learning, as discussed and defined in this lesson, is
a) listening to a source of information.
b) seeing and hearing a presentation of factual information.
c) discovering truth after an extensive search.
d) discovering information and making desired responses to it.

20 The goal of learning is described in this lesson as
a) using truth as a base for making life choices and guiding actions.
b) building a framework for life's decisions that is intellectually, socially, and psychologically feasible.
c) the acquisition of the knowledge, attitudes, and skills necessary for a full and productive life.
d) the development of man in his total makeup: knowledge, attitudes, and skills.

answers to study questions

6 b) learners change consistent with the truth.
   d) learners put truth into action.
   e) learners discover and respond to information.

1 a Your answer. Many people say something like this: Learning is receiving information, such as a lesson, from someone.
   b Your answer. Again, many people believe that teaching involves dispensing information to a listener or listeners.

7 a 1) Knowledge.
   b 2) Attitude.
   c 3) Behavior.
   d 2) Attitude.
   e 1) Knowledge.
   f 3) Behavior.
   g 1) Knowledge.
   h 2) Attitude.
   i 3) Behavior.
   j 3) Behavior.
   k 1) Knowledge.
   l 2) Attitude.

2 a 1) Transfer learning.
   b 2) Discovery learning.
   c 3) Your answer.

8 a 1) Rote memory.
   b 2) Restatement.
   c 3) Comprehension.
   d 4) Application.
   e 2) Restatement.
   f 1) Rote memory.

g 4) Application.
h 3) Comprehension.
i 3) Comprehension.
j 4) Application.
k 1) Rote memory.
l 2) Restatement.
m 2) Restatement.
n 1) Rote memory.
o 3) Comprehension.
p 3) Comprehension.

3 Your answer. I would expect the learner in Pierre's class to learn more than a learner in Brigette's class. The learner in Pierre's class, being involved in the process, would tend to identify with the lesson and it would be more meaningful to him than if he were a mere spectator.

9 a 3) Through practice.
b 1) Through the senses.
c 2) Through involvement.
d 4) Through problem solving.
e 1) Through the senses.
f 3) Through practice.
g 4) Through problem solving.
h 2) Through involvement.

4 a 1) Transfer learning.
b 2) Discovery learning.
c 2) Discovery learning.
d 1) Transfer learning.
e 2) Discovery learning.
f 1) Transfer learning.
g 2) Discovery learning.
h 1) Transfer learning.

10 a False.
   b True.
   c False.
   d True.
   e True.
   f False.
   g False.
   h True.

5 Disciples are to be taught obedience to the commandments Jesus gave.

LESSON 5

Developing and Learning

Juan works as a farmer. He works hard in his fields preparing the soil, planting the seeds, spreading fertilizers, and spraying insecticides. His carrots, beans, squash, tomatoes, and other vegetables seem to grow faster and bigger than those grown by the other farmers in the area. Customers at the local market are willing to pay more for his produce because of its superior quality.

Juan understands an important growth principle: Given the benefit of favorable conditions, the life in the seed can be helped to develop to its maximum growth potential. *Care* and *favorable conditions* produce plants that reflect health and vitality as they ripen and mature. Juan has learned to recognize signs of proper development. He knows just what to do at each stage of growth to stimulate progress from tiny sprouts, to tender young plants, and on to fully ripened produce.

You may have seen that the same growth principle which makes Juan a successful farmer applies in the realm of spiritual life. In this lesson you will learn facts about learners that will help you to encourage their growth and development potential. By creating favorable learning conditions, recognizing the special needs of learners at each developmental level, and adjusting your nurturing strategy to respond to these special needs, you can stimulate the

learning process. May you be sensitive not only to facts about learners but also to the leading and timing of the Holy Spirit, the Master Teacher, as you apply the knowledge you gain.

lesson outline

Understanding Human Development
Characteristics of Learners

lesson objectives

When you finish this lesson you should be able to:

- Explain how humans grow and develop, identifying the major periods of human life.

- Describe characteristics of learners in childhood, adolescence, and adulthood, and in the subperiods of each one of these major periods.

- Discuss factors which affect human personality.

125

learning activities

1. Read each one of the lesson objectives and note the major divisions of the lesson in the outline.

2. Work through the lesson development as usual. As you do the study questions, be sure to write your own responses before you turn to the answers we have given. Take the self-test when you have finished and check your answers.

key words

abstractions	inquisitive	perceptibly
competitive	intimacy	senility
fascination	intricate	symbolism
hygiene	intriguing	temporal

lesson development

UNDERSTANDING HUMAN DEVELOPMENT

How People Grow

Objective 1. *Choose statements which describe correctly how people grow.*

Success in building relationships and in effective teaching depends to a large extent on our understanding of the nature of human beings. To understand ourselves and those we seek to nurture in spiritual growth, we must study human development.

People grow in many ways. As soon as life begins, we start growing physically. Our bodies contine to grow for a number of years, reaching maximum stature in early adulthood. We also grow intellectually, emotionally, socially, and spiritually. Growth in these four areas can continue long after the physical growth of the body

126

has stopped. In fact growth in the nonphysical areas can continue throughout life until either death, senility or physical deterioration disrupts the capacity for growth.

Growth in each of these five areas or facets of life is important. To be properly developed in all five is to be whole. Wholeness is realized when we achieve an ideal balance in each of these areas. Imbalance exists when a person fails to develop properly in one or more of these basic areas of life, or when one area is developed to the neglect of the others. The goal of Christian nurture is wholeness—proper development in each area of life.

Christians often place high priority on spiritual growth. We value spiritual growth because the Christ-life is eternal. Other areas of human life are temporal and cease with death, but the spirit of man lives on after death and returns to God. Therefore, in Christian nurture we place great emphasis on spiritual development.

While growth is natural, we should not assume that growth in wholeness is automatic. It must be encouraged and nurtured. Teachers, as well as other Christians, have opportunities to facilitate growth.

1 Circle the letters preceding the statements that are TRUE.
a People grow physically, intellectually, emotionally, socially, and spiritually.
b To the Christian, growth in each area of life is important.
c Wholeness is when an ideal balance is achieved in each potential area of human growth.
d Christian nurture places the highest priority on physical growth.
e Christian growth is natural and comes automatically.
f Growth in nonphysical areas should continue throughout life.

Major Periods of Life

Objective 2. *Correctly identify developmental periods of life.*

We commonly identify three major periods of human life: *childhood, adolescence* or *youth,* and *adulthood. Childhood* refers to that period of life from birth to about age eleven or twelve years. *Adolescence* refers to the period of life from about age twelve to about eighteen or nineteen. *Adulthood*, the longest period of life, begins at about twenty years and continues until death. Since many people live to be very old, this period may extend to as much as two-thirds or three-fourths of a lifetime.

Have you noticed that as people pass through these human development periods their abilities, needs, and characteristics change? A newborn baby is very different from what he will be at age ten. A young adult in his early twenties is different from an adult of sixty or seventy. It is evident that three broad groupings cannot describe accurately the many stages of human development. Consequently, we divide each of these periods into three subdivisions for a more accurate description of the changes characteristic of each substage of growth.

1. *Childhood*, the first major period of life, is subdivided in three categories: early, middle, and later childhood. *Early childhood* describes the period from birth to about age five or six. In many societies children begin school at the close of this period. *Middle childhood* is the period from age five or six to age nine or ten years. *Later childhood* covers the period from age ten to the beginning of adolescence at about age twelve.

2. *Adolescence*, the second major period of life, is likewise divided into three segments: early, middle, and later adolescence. *Early adolescence* includes ages twelve to about fifteen. In many countries adolescents in this bracket attend middle school or junior high school. *Middle adolescence* includes adolescents from fifteen to seventeen years. Middle adolescents in many cultures attend secondary or high school classes. *Later adolescence* includes youths from about seventeen to nineteen years. Graduation from secondary school usually comes at the beginning of later adolescence.

3. *Adulthood*, the third and final major period of life, is also subdivided into early, middle, and later categories. *Early adulthood* extends from about age twenty to about age thirty-five or forty. It

is a period of many beginnings: vocation, home, and family, to name a few. *Middle adulthood* covers the period from about thirty-five or forty to sixty or sixty-five years of age. This segment of time is characterized by completion of some of one's earlier goals, for example, getting established in a community and getting the children raised, educated, and prepared for adulthood. *Later adulthood* reaches from sixty or sixty-five years on to the end of life.

Some years ago an insurance firm used three categories to describe the major periods of life. The childhood and adolescent years were referred to as the "learning period." Early and middle adulthood were called the "earning period." And later adulthood was named the "yearning period." Perhaps there is a lesson in this for you and me as we try to make the most of our time and talents in nurturing Christian growth. May the facts we study here inspire us to apply the sowing-reaping principles employed by Juan so that we can help develop healthy, spiritual growth in people.

Differences of characteristics from one period to the next are much greater in childhood and adolescence than in adulthood. Neither the major divisions nor the subdivisions within them, however, are clearly fixed. Each person develops at a different rate.

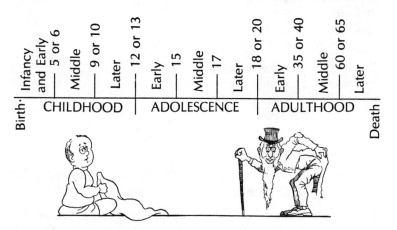

MAJOR DIVISIONS AND SUBDIVISIONS OF HUMAN LIFE

2-7 Circle the letter in front of the appropriate age level for each of the people described below.

2 A boy who is eleven years old
a) Middle childhood
b) Later childhood ⟋
c) Middle adolescence

3 A twenty-seven year old lady
a) Infancy
b) Later adolescence
c) Early adulthood

4 A man of seventy years
a) Later adulthood
b) Middle adulthood
c) Later adolescence

5 A girl of three years
a) Early childhood
b) Middle childhood
c) Early adolescence

6 A lad of fourteen years
a) Early childhood
b) Early adolescence
c) Early adulthood

7 A person of nineteen years
a) Middle adulthood
b) Middle adolescence
c) Later adolescence

Personality Development

Objective 3. *Choose statements which identify three factors that affect the development of human personality.*

You will see that when people have balanced growth in the five areas of life mentioned above, a state of wholeness exists. And you will learn that as people pass through various development periods, their needs, abilities, and characteristics change. First, we want to consider the parallel development of *personality* and the factors that influence it most strongly. This brief preview will give us insight into yet another factor that influences one's learning capability.

People in the same age span are generally alike in many ways. They tend to follow similar patterns of growth and development. Yet no one individual can be considered typical: no one conforms exactly to a list of general characteristics. Each person is unique, having his own particular temperament, character, and personality, but these are developed and modified through experience, nurture, and the learning process.

Personality is a term which refers to the total of what a person is. It includes one's thoughts, actions, attitudes, traits, temperament, and character.

Human personality is affected by complex forces over a long period of time. Here we will discuss three factors which affect personality development: 1) heredity, 2) environment, and 3) will.

1. *Heredity.* The specific traits which we inherit from our parents are referred to as heredity. Body size and shape, the color of hair and eyes, dispositions, and intellectual abilities are a few examples of the qualities which make up our personalities. Much attention has been given to the differences between people in their intellectual abilities due to heredity. These mental abilities seem to determine within broad limits the extent to which an individual has the capacity to learn. This heredity factor is especially seen in the way children learn and develop. The capacity for growth and development in each area of life is part of people's natural endowment. However, due to the unique combination of traits which affect personality development which are received through heredity, each individual will grow and develop in a manner which is different from anyone else.

2. *Environment.* Environment refers to our surroundings. People develop in physical settings that have limiting and determining effects on their development. For example, life in a nomad's tent and life

in a crowded apartment complex have different influences on growing children. Imagine, for instance, the difference between rural children who can dig, run, jump, explore fields, and engage in work and play activities in their physical environment, and city children who live in crowded apartment buildings and play on crowded streets and alleys in an asphalt jungle. The social environment, which also affects people's development, includes such things as: neighborhoods in which they live, occupation and education, family income, quality of available schools, opportunities available for recreational, cultural, and religious activity, and other factors. Culture is also a part of our environment. Every culture has established its own values and teaches conduct based on these values. Environment provides both limitations and opportunities to develop our mental abilities. We generally prefer an environment which provides broad opportunities for development to one which provides narrow, limited opportunities.

3. *Will*. People's wills also affect their personality development. They have been given the power to choose. They may either choose to take advantage of the opportunities for development which are available to them, or they may choose to ignore or neglect these opportunities. Some people believe that the will is more important to personality development than either one's inherited mental capacity or his environmental opportunities.

8 Circle the letter in front of each TRUE statement.

a Every person is born with the capacity to grow, develop, and learn.

b Intellectual ability is one area in which all people are equal.

c Where a person lives has nothing to do with his ability to grow, develop, and learn.

d People's surroundings can either provide specific opportunities to foster growth, development, and learning or to hinder each development.

e A person's desire to grow, develop, and learn has a definite effect on whether he will make progress in these areas.

f One is the victim of his heredity, environment, and will; therefore, it is useless to attempt to modify, develop, or otherwise improve his condition in life.

CHARACTERISTICS OF LEARNERS

Objective 4. *Select learning activities which are appropriate for learners in each of the major divisions of life.*

Learning is affected by growth. However, as one begins to develop, the learning which he acquires becomes the basis for continued development. The first major stage of development we will focus our attention on is that of childhood. Beginning in a very helpless state, the child grows through various identifiable stages. By the time the child has progressed to adolescence, he has developed perceptibly in the physical, social, intellectual, and spiritual realms. In this section, you will study the various stages of growth, and you will find characteristics common to these stages.

Early Childhood

The period of life from birth to the beginning of a child's formal schooling brings many developmental changes. Some have suggested that more development and learning takes place in this period than any other period of life.

Physically

Throughout infancy and early childhood, people experience very rapid physical growth. At birth, a child is quite small and helpless. He must depend on his mother and others for every need. But by the time the child enters school, he has grown considerably. He has learned to turn over in bed, sit up, stand, walk, and run. The rapid growth of this period results from the development of the large muscles. These large muscles control the ability for large movements of the body which do not require much coordination or precision. At this age the small muscles one needs for fine movements are not yet fully developed. Therefore the child is not able to perform delicate operations such as tracing lines, cutting on lines, or coloring within lines of a picture. This control comes with time. Much of the child's development is evidenced through play. Movement activities such as running, jumping, throwing, kicking or hitting a ball, and stacking

133

blocks are typical physical development activities for small children. This means that small children must be kept occupied with movement activities. They cannot sit for long periods without becoming restless since their attention span is very short. Because they are active, they tire quickly and need a balance between physical action and creative involvement which is less demanding on their physical bodies.

Mentally

Early childhood is a time of mental discovery. The child discovers through his senses. This is why he tries to touch everything within his reach and frequently puts things into his mouth. He is discovering and therefore needs the protective care of an older person, since he has not learned the dangers of swallowing or touching harmful objects. Small children tend to be inquisitive and ask many questions. This is their way of exploring the world around them.

In this period, children are learning to use language as a tool to express themselves. From the first spoken words, their ability to use language develops rather rapidly. By the time children reach school age, they have vocabularies of about 1,000 words, depending on their home environment and cultural influence. Their ability with language is usually limited to speaking. They have not yet learned to read or write. If you teach children of this age, you will need to use words they understand. They have literal understanding of what they are told; therefore, you should choose words which give your exact meaning.

During this early period of development, children's ability to focus attention on a single idea is very limited. At about two or three years the attention span is often no longer than two or three minutes, but by the time they begin their schooling this may have increased to seven or even ten minutes. Because of this fact, teachers should plan learning activities which recognize this time span. Activities should change before the learners' attention turns to other things.

Quite commonly small children have vivid imaginations. They have the ability to bypass reality and live in a world of "let's pretend." This can be used to help teach many truths. In this same time frame, many parents challenge their children to memorize simple poetry, songs and even short Scripture passages. Children's performance in this activity is amazing because of their high motivation and because of their unusual ability to retain what they learn.

At this early age children are usually emotionally secure in the presence of their own families but they may be fearful of the unfamiliar and unknown. You can enhance their security by becoming a true friend.

Spiritually

In this early stage of life, the child believes everything he is told and is easily influenced. He is impressionable and wants to do what is right, especially when this is properly reinforced with loving approval. While his ability to understand God is limited, the small child can understand certain basic spiritual truths. He can understand that God is a special friend; the church is a special place; and that God loves and cares for him. The small child can express loving worship to God in response to the warm feelings he experiences when he is learning about God. He can easily memorize very basic Scripture passages. He responds to love and can easily understand and respond to God's love.

9 Circle the letter in front of each activity which would be appropriate for learners at the early childhood level.
a) Sing happy songs about God.
b) Require the class to sit quietly through the period.
c) Require the children to play with others all of the time.
d) Include activities that require movement and intersperse short quiet times.
e) Since the children are so young. avoid talking about God.
f) Allow the children to play along part of the time.
g) Put things up high so the children can see them but not touch them.
h) Talk about God as the child's loving friend.
i) Teach the class to memorize the Lord's Prayer.
j) Provide things that go with the lesson for the children to feel and handle.

10 Carefully observe one or two children between the ages of three and six. Write in your notebook the characteristics you discover. Compare your discoveries with the characteristics described in this text.

Middle Childhood

The beginning of formal schooling is usually considered to be the distinguishing mark between early and middle childhood. This period marks the beginning of many developments in children's lives. Growth and development continue to be rapid.

Physically

During the middle childhood years children are very active. They like vigorous physical activity but they tire quickly. Much of their energy is expended in growing. Their physical growth is irregular. They may grow very rapidly for a short period; then their growth may slow noticeably for some time. During this stage the heart develops more slowly than the rest of the body. Because of this they tire easily. However, the coordination and muscular control children need for organized games develops, and their activities become purposeful. They enjoy making things, particularly toys and items to enhance their play.

Mentally

Children's attention span in this period has increased and they can now concentrate on a particular idea for 10 to 15 minutes. Although their reason and discrimination are not fully developed, they are, nevertheless, keen observers who often notice specific details. Probing interest in searching for information is a normal characteristic of their expanding knowledge. Frequently they overrate their own knowledge.

Children are learning to read and write now and their vocabularies are increasing. As a result they may frequently express themselves with words that they either mispronounce or use incorrectly.

They tend to think literally and have not yet learned the use of symbolism, abstractions, and generalizations. They have good memories and can eaily memorize songs, poems, and Bible verses appropriate for their developmental level.

In the middle childhood years children tend to be insecure emotionally. It is not uncommon for them to express themselves by crying. Their social world is broadening, and they often interpret this as threatening to the security they have known in early life in the loving environment of their families and homes. They need loving acceptance and approval from adults such as parents, teachers, and other respected adult leaders.

Socially

Since children are now in school, their social views are broadening. Their friendships have expanded beyond their families to include other children and teachers. They make friends of both sexes easily and learn to function as parts of groups. They learn to cooperate by giving and by sharing in responsibilities. Their focus in play begins to change from themselves to group activities. Their ethic of fairness and right and wrong is developing, and they are easily hurt if they believe they have been treated unfairly.

Spiritually

In middle childhood children possess tender consciences, implicit faith, and the desire to obey. They are spiritually inclined and readily respond to truth about God. They learn well by stories and especially enjoy Bible stories. Bible stories can be used both to teach moral concepts and lay the foundation for a future chronological understanding of the Bible. Children's consciences are developing, and right and wrong actions affect their peace of mind. They look to adults for standards of behavior and quickly follow their examples. Parents have a powerful influence here, as well as an awesome resonsibility. Since teachers are highly respected, also, their spiritual example cannot be overemphasized. It must be regarded seriously by teachers of all levels of learners, but especially so for children whose parents are not Christians. Non-Christian parents very likely do not reinforce spiritual values in the home life. Often children in the middle childhood group are ready to make personal commitments to Christ. This readiness is often dependent on the home experience, attendance at church, and the meaningful teaching and personal example of the teacher.

11 Which of the following would be appropriate teaching activities for a Christian nurture class for the middle childhood age group? Write 1) on the line in front of a statement if you agree that the activity it suggests is appropriate, and 2) if you disagree.

....**a** Teach the class to memorize the books of the Bible in the correct order.

....**b** Schedule long periods of physical activity and emphasize the need for physical fitness.

....**c** Make frequent use of the storytelling method of teaching.

....**d** Consider that your responsibility for influencing the child is limited to the actual lessons you teach during class hours.

....**e** Enrich the stories you tell with abstractions and symbolism.

....**f** Talk specifically to the children about receiving Christ as their personal Savior.

....**g** Play learning games that help mold the children's conscience by having to make right and wrong choices.

12 Carefully observe two or three children between the ages of six and nine. Write in your notebook the characteristics you discover. Compare what you discover with the characteristics described in the lesson content in this section.

Later Childhood

The preadolescent years are an exciting and challenging part of life. Children's potential in all areas of life is unlimited. They are active and noisy and they enjoy life. Their interests are many and varied.

Physically

In later childhood children seem to have boundless energy. They are stronger now than they were in earlier childhood, but their physical growth rate is slower than in previous years. They have healthy appetites and need plenty of food, sunshine, fresh air, and rest. Their muscle control is improving, and they have greatly improved coordination for more intricate work. They have a tendency to neglect proper physical care and hygiene. Consequently, they may tend to be careless about grooming and the care of their personal possessions, not treating clothing, books, and other items with care. Their abounding energy can be turned into worthwhile and helpful activities if they have the proper motivation and guidance.

Mentally

At this age, preadolescents are inquisitive and desire to explore and discover. They are beginning to observe accurately and reason logically. They are alert and eager to learn new truths. They enjoy collecting items, from books to posters, stamps, bottle caps, stones, and insects. Their fascination with things often leads them to take apart and rebuild such things as mechanical toys or clocks and watches. They usually read easily and enjoy adventure stories. Books about missionaries or foreign places are frequently intriguing. Preadolescents usually identify with the hero of the story. They have the ability to memorize very quickly and are beginning to understand concepts. They may be able to repeat concepts without fully understanding them. Symbolisms need to be clarified with literal explanations and examples. While they are gaining self-control, preadolescents' emotions are sensitive and they respond quickly to supposed slights. They are quick to argue and are easily disturbed; however, they soon cool off and rarely hold grudges. Preadolescents tend to jump to conclusions based on limited facts. They need to be taught to gather more information before they come to premature conclusions.

In later childhood, children are usually sensitive and fearful in spite of fearless, bold fronts. They have the tendency to hide their true feelings, which often go unexpressed. They are fun loving, have a developing sense of humor, and enjoy jokes and cartoons.

Socially

Preadolescents begin to seek independence though they frequently retreat to the security of parental help. They are conscious of the likes of others their own age, that is, what is "in" or popular. They are joiners, organizing and joining groups and clubs among their peers. They admire people and identify with them, drawing their sense of values from them. They have a growing tendency to relate more to peers and less to adult leaders. Preadolescents are competitive and eagerly enter either group or individual contests. They participate with enthusiasm and consider the outcome to be serious. However, at this age the sexes often separate themselves socially. Girls usually are not permitted to join a boys' club, for example.

Spiritually

Since those in this period of life are "hero worshipers," they should be challenged by the biblical heroes of faith. Quite frequently preadolescents are ready for salvation, and their relationship with God should not be taken for granted. During this important period, we must be sure to provide teaching about God's plan of salvation, including the consequences of sin and the need to confess sin and seek forgiveness. This is an appropriate time to teach spiritual concepts of doctrine, meaningful Christian living, and Bible chronology. Preadolescents are capable of understanding spiritual truth when it is presented with an abundance of practical examples in ways that foster discovery and adventure. Ample Scripture memorization should be included in their learning and experience. You should emphasize the value of developing good habits of regular Bible reading and prayer, as well as Christian living and service.

13 In view of the characteristics of the late childhood period, which of the following would provide appropriate opportunities to nurture effective Christian growth? Write 1) on the line in front of each statement if you agree that the activity suggested would nurture Christian growth, and 2) if you disagree.

....**a** A camping trip for children sponsored by the church

....**b** A Bible memorization club

....**c** A lecture series on the "evidence for biblical inspiration"

....**d** A special class which studies church doctrine

....**e** A reading library at the church to provide appropriate and exciting stories and reading materials

....**f** A children's evangelistic crusade

....**g** A panel discussion of the abuses of alcohol

14 Observe carefully two or three children between the ages of ten and twelve. Write in your notebook the characteristics you discover. Compare your discoveries with the characteristics described in the lesson content in this section.

Adolescence

During childhood, change and growth patterns are more predictable for various age groups than they are in the last two major stages of development. During the adolescence phase, individuals may vary a great deal in their development physically, socially, spiritually, and mentally, even though they may be very close to the same age. It is difficult to predict accurately that all adolescents of the same age will behave in the same way. When studying this growth stage, we will look at trends of development rather than fixed phases of change which occur at specific ages. Of course there will be many similarities between individuals of the same age, but in many ways they will be very different than they were in the childhood phase.

Early Adolescence

Adolescence is a transition period between childhood and adulthood. This transition includes a change from being dependent on parents to independence, and from simple, childlike trust and acceptance to independent decision making. As we discuss adolescence let us remember that those in this period may be referred to correctly as *adolescents, young people, youths,* or *teenagers.*

Early adolescence, as we have seen, includes roughly ages twelve to fifteen. It is a time of great change for young people, especially in terms of their physical changes and the social adjustments required by these changes. In many societies adolescents in this category attend middle or junior high school.

Physically

Adolescents continue to grow and develop physically. Girls nearly reach their adult height by early adolescence. They grow to this level of physical maturity from two to four years earlier than boys. Vital organs grow rapidly: the heart doubles in size, the lungs grow, and the glands become more active. The uneven growth rate of bones may make one appear to be awkward, and this can cause some embarrassment. Vocal cords lengthen and adolescents frequently have difficulty controlling their voices.

Early adolescence also signals the coming of puberty: the period in life which brings about the development of the sex glands and sexual functions. Girls' bodies begin to assume their adult, feminine shape and boys' physiques become more masculine. In some societies these changes are celebrated by certain rites of passage or ceremonies which recognize the change from childhood to young "adulthood."

Mentally

The mental abilities of teenagers are growing. They are capable of serious thinking and are often critical and doubtful. This is a wholesome development of the ability for independent reasoning.

142

In their quest for independence, teenagers may become severely critical of themselves. They often find it difficult to accept their abilities, appearance, background, families or any other personal uniqueness and may even reject them. They also have a changing awareness of their own self-concepts. In this period, young people have a tendency to be overly idealistic as they begin to exercise their new-found powers of logical thought.

Socially

During early adolescence parental influence lessens, and parent-teen relations may be strained. The peer group has strong attraction. Youths in this period want very much to be accepted. To be popular is one of their primary goals. The drastic changes teenagers face at this time make them vulnerable to feelings of inadequacy and inability to face the increasing changes and challenges of life. Yet, in spite of this external drive for independence and identification with peer groups, teenagers often feel lonely and desperately need reassurance that they are loved, accepted, and understood by those who are mature and stable in life, expecially by parents. Under peer pressure to conform to the expectations of the "in" group, early adolescents are tempted to experiment with a multitude of new experiences: drugs, sex, drink, the occult, false religions, and anti-Christian teachings. It is a crucial period for adolescents, parents, and society.

Spiritually

The frustrations and doubts that early teenagers experience in other areas of life may carry over to the spiritual area, also. Youths who dislike themselves may find it difficult to believe that the God who created them is loving and kind. They need help and understanding in this crucial period. Parents and teachers must accept them as they are and endeavor to build a relationship with them in which trust can develop. As you relate to them both in and out of class, you can help them see that they need not walk alone in their struggles. With Jesus Christ in control of their lives they can have

His power to help them lead victorious lives and His presence to encourage, comfort, and support them. You can help them face life's problems as you teach them to direct their lives according to biblical principles.

Middle Adolescence

Middle adolescence includes the period from about fifteen to about age eighteen. In most urban societies, middle adolescents attend secondary or senior high school; others attend vocational training schools. In traditional societies, youths of this age generally enter the work force and help to support their families. Let's take a closer look at four specific areas of development.

Physically

Middle adolescents continue to grow. While girls in general tend to reach their adult height in early adolescence, boys' development continues on into middle and even later adolescence. Both girls and boys demonstrate change toward physical maturity. Boys become more muscular and better coordinated. They have considerable strength and stamina. Boys begin to develop beards and begin the lifelong task of shaving. Girls continue developing into their adult, feminine physical identity. Middle adolescents enjoy action sports or activities, and they participate with a will, demonstrating both good form and excellent condition. Both girls and boys are concerned about their physical appearance, and they spend much time in grooming and personal care.

Mentally

The serious and critical thinking begun in early adolescence is maturing in middle adolescence. Reason and judgments are continuing to develop. No longer will another's answers satisfy. Adolescents individually must solve their own intellectual problems. At this time they begin to focus their attention on skills and interests that may be suitable for their respective vocations.

The idealism which young people develop in early adolescence may become even more pronounced at this time. The basis of adolescents' judgment is often what appears to be logical to them rather than what may appear to be realistic to an older, more mature person. During this phase of growth, young people may have difficulties distinguishing between their own idealistic ideas and the realities of the world around them.

Socially

This is the time of life for the development of social awareness and the acceptance of one's place in society. Probably one of the biggest issues for adolescents to cope with is that of personal identity. They have developed self concepts in which each sees himself as a totally different person from anyone else. It is a concept of self-uniqueness. Each becomes aware of his personal differences and characteristics such as likes and dislikes, talents, goals, aptitude, and the strength and purpose to guide his own destiny.

Quite naturally adolescents have an increasing awareness of their destiny and the future. These are new feelings. Often young people may experience a state of confusion which may lead to times of unnecessary self-consciousness. Their behavior may become inconsistent and unpredictable during this time of transition.

Spiritually

The searching, keen minds of adolescents may lead them at times to doubt absolute values or even the existence of God. They may ask such questions as: "What is the meaning of existence?" "What is of lasting value?" "What is absolute authority?" You can channel the questions of adolescents toward investigation of biblical truth, the claims of God on man's life, and the value of biblical principles as a basis for daily living. You, the teacher, can direct learners toward finding God's will for their lives, and you can challenge them to a complete commitment of their lives to Christ. You can lead them to see that the answers to life's greatest problems can be solved as they seek God's help in prayer, meaningful Bible study, and consistent Christian service.

Later Adolescence

The years from eighteen to twenty are the final years of adolescence. They bring young people to the threshold of adulthood, the next major period of life. In modern urban societies this period corresponds to the time when many young people begin the final phase of their educational program at the college or university level. In predominantly rural societies young people are generally occupied with the problem of finding jobs to help support their families.

Physically

Late teenagers are moving toward the peak of their physical strength. Most of the physical growth has ended by this time, but body tone becomes better and physical fitness tends to be excellent. Generally, however, the changes in the physical body at this point are less apparent than during previous phases of adolescence.

Mentally

After many years of schooling, later adolescents are now reaching maturity in their intellectual abilities. With some experience and practical application of knowledge behind them, they demonstrate responsible decision-making. They tend to be idealistic, but this is becoming tempered with some realism gained through experience.

As adolescents involve themselves increasingly in their adult roles and begin to assume adult responsibilities, they begin to develop a point of view seasoned with the realities of life. While they may continue to harbor idealistic ideas and dreams, they are able to adapt their thinking increasingly to the demands of the environment in which they live and work.

Socially

In some countries, as secondary schooling comes to an end, adolescents are faced with the future: should they continue their education or should they locate a job, move to their own dwelling places, and begin a new phase of life on their own? In others, the issues are clearer, for one may not necessarily leave his family, establish his own independent residence, and seek his own future.

Adolescents encounter another dimension of development: the emergence of a sense of loyalty. This can be seen throughout adolescence, but it seems to culminate in this stage. As they are reaching a state of sexual maturity, they are also developing a sense of loyalty and fidelity. This sense of loyalty prepares each to commit himself to an adult pattern of life and the likelihood of taking a marriage partner.

Emerging from childhood into adulthood results in many changes in the individual. From dependence on parents to self direction in responsible decision making, one blossoms into a person who is prepared to enter the adult role in life and seek the intimacy of a marriage relationship. At this point one can receive a new sense of self; he can also receive a perception of his future and the destiny yet to be fulfilled during the adult stages of his life.

Spiritually

The educational, social, and intellectual background of many later adolescents is such today that they seek to involve themselves increasingly with issues which are "relevant" to them. If we design our approach to nurturing with this in mind we can challenge adolescents to find answers to many of the pressing social, spiritual, and moral issues they face daily. Later adolescents are not content with traditional answers; they want to come to grips with the issues that affect their responses to a world with few standards. You may have to change your approach or prepare more fully, but teaching formats which include discussion groups, buzz groups, and panel discussions, to name a few, will meet with grateful responses.

15 In view of the foregoing characteristics, which of the following are appropriate Christian nurturing activities for adolescents? Write 1) on the line in front of statements that are approprite and 2) in front of those that would not be appropriate.

....**a** A series of lessons on self-acceptance

....**b** A series of stories about Bible heroes

....**c** A series of lessons on the Christian view of love, courtship, and marriage

....**d** A series of sermons condemning the care of the physical body as unnecessary vanity

....**e** A series of lessons on the practical application of biblical teaching to every day life situations

....**f** A series of talks on biblical teachings about interpersonal relationships

....**g** A series of lessons on current theories of behavior and one's need to conform his behavior to the expectations of society

....**h** A series of talks on parent-teen relationships to be attended by parents and their adolescent children

....**i** A series of lessons on finding God's will

....**j** A series of lectures showing the uselessness and unimportance of reason and mental pursuits

Adulthood

The final major stage we will consider is that of adulthood. This phase of life may cover a span of time greater than half a century. Previously, the childhood and adolescent stages were seen as *learning periods*. Adulthood may be labeled as the age when most people begin *earning*. The last period of adulthood may be characterized by *yearning*, looking back wistfully over the experiences that have enriched life and given it meaning. This study of adulthood has been divided into three phases with each phase representing characteristic events in life which are likely to occur during certain years. However, you should keep in mind that chronological age does not necessarily mean that everyone at a particular age will be experiencing the same things as others in that age group. People are now changing by choice rather than by solely physical development in many areas. They do continue to change physically, but the change is not as rapid as one may see in the childhood and adolescent stages.

Early Adulthood

Early adulthood, which begins around age twenty, is characterized by the desire to find a marriage partner, establish a home, and raise children. Young adults begin to work at their occupations, establish themselves in their communities, and educate their children.

Physically

The word *adult* means "fully developed and mature." The adult has reached his maximum physical growth. His strength, which reaches its peak in this period, begins to wane in later adulthood. It is appropriate that at the time when people face tasks requiring strength, stamina, and good health, they reach the state of greatest physical development.

Mentally

Young adults, having undergone intensive training and having experienced some of the realities of responsible decision-making, have seemingly unlimited intellectual capacity. They are sharp and idealistic, their reason is maturing and their interests are becoming more specialized. Many of the intellectual doubts of their adolescence are settled, and they tend to be stable, responsible people.

Socially

In adulthood family relationships continue to be of utmost importance. Young adults develop relationships based on intimacy. Their relationships with parents develop, and they tend to enjoy a mature level of interaction. They no longer need to depend on parents to make decisions for them or to approve of the decisions they make. Out of mature love for their parents healthy and whole relationships emerge. Young adults also seek to associate with others who share common goals and interests. Friendships may evolve out of their relationships from such areas as work, church, neighborhood, and schools. They are aware of the need to be integrated into the community in which they live, rather than be isolated from it.

Spiritually

For those who have been nurtured in Christian homes during their childhood and adolescent years, adulthood is a time for the application and reinforcement of the lessons they have learned previously. Adulthood for them should be a time of active involvement in Christian service. Some adults, however, have not been prepared for Christian service, either because of non-Christian background or inadequate Christian nurturing. In any case, all adults need to be encouraged to keep in mind spiritual priorities. As young parents study the Bible in depth, they need to be challenged to set up a family altar and create an atmosphere in which wholesome spiritual life can be nurtured. Without the concern of nurturing leaders, young adults can be permitted to be absorbed into the busyness of modern life to the exclusion of spiritual life.

Middle Adulthood

Around the ages of 35 to 40 adults enter another identifiable stage which is often referred to as "middle age." Middle adults have reached many of their earlier objectives. This calls for some major adjustments.

The children have grown up, completed their education, and in many modern societies, left home. The activities that involved family finances, time, and energies during these fleeting years have ended. Now parents may experience feelings of emptiness and loneliness. They may appear at times to be "adrift." The husband and wife may also have to make adjustments in their relationship to each other. Middle adults may question their occupational goals and the direction of their lives. They may even make major decisions to change their lifestyles.

150

One of the rewarding features of this period is grandchildren. They tend to bless the lives of the grandparents and give new purpose to their relationship. During this time many adults face the prospect of adjusting to the death of parents. This brings about the need for additional adjustment.

Physically

Middle age brings physical changes to both men and women. Men who enter adulthood with superb physiques may tend to develop the middle age spread, gaining excessive weight as they lose muscle tone. Or, becoming aware of aging and the loss of strength, they may be motivated to begin "reconditioning programs." Women lose their reproductive function during the middle years. They, too, may tend to lose muscle tone, gain weight, and show some of the marks of aging: greying hair and wrinkled skin. Many women today are engaging in exercise and physical fitness programs, to restore lost body tone and regain some of the vigor they enjoyed in earlier years.

Mentally

In middle adulthood people's intellectual powers are devoted to production, and they are quietly persistent. The judgment of middle adults is generally sound and dependable, and this is reflected in a sense of self-confidence and feelings of competence. This is the period in life for achievement and full production. Perhaps you have noticed that the managers and executives in many occupations are middle aged people. This is so because of their experience and proved performance.

Socially

During middle adulthood, whole, mature adults tend to develop a sense of caring which is expressed by their concern for others. They may wish to take care of others and share their knowledge and experience with them. Satisfaction and contentment come through nurturing and teaching others. Middle adults frequently feel a strong desire to share the truths which have come to guide and bless their lives with their children. They wish to perpetuate the customs and rituals, seeking to preserve and protect these enriching experiences which have sustained them throughout their lives.

Spiritually

At this stage in life there can be a tendency toward materialism and busyness with matters of secondary importance. Quite frequently these important matters crowd out the spiritual dimension of people's lives, robbing them of time, strength, and true vision. In contrast, however, faith in middle adulthood can be deep and personal.

Middle adults, being in their prime intellectually in terms of life experiences, need to be fed spiritual food consistent with their mature status, challenged to meaningful Christian service, and utilized wherever possible. Lessons geared to nurture this level should be challenging, well prepared, and capably presented. Not only do those pillars of the church need solid spiritual meat but also to be challenged to apply the lessons of their lifetime in practical ways.

Later Adulthood

Later adulthood begins around sixty to sixty-five years of age. In the final stage of this period, adults come to the realization that advancing years leave little time to fulfill their hopes and dreams. Grandchildren and great grandchildren now become an important part of their families, and they often feel the need to prepare the younger generation for the future. These people are faced with the fact that death is approaching; therefore, they characteristically make preparation for it.

Physically

As adults reach maturity and grow older, they often develop ailments with accompanying aches and pains. These physical problems alert one to the need to make both mental and physical adjustments. They must accept the fact that their strength has limits and that the total person can only be as productive as health permits.

In many places today activities are planned which take into consideration the physical limitations of "senior citizens."

Mentally

As adults leave the labor market at the end of middle adulthood, they represent the combined training, acquired knowledge and experience of over one-half century. They have made their contributions, directed their generation, and completed their vocational courses successfully. Older adults are a valuable asset to their families, churches, and communities for the wise experienced counsel they can give. Their accumulated knowledge and experienced wisdom can contribute to the development of those in all other periods of life.

Socially

Later adulthood brings people to the closing years of life. One of the chief virtues which graces life at this season is wisdom. Mature people are able to review their lives and derive a sense of meaningfulness and worthwhileness from them. They are able to face objectively both their successes and failures without either leaving them with an undue sense of pride or despair. To the younger person, they project an aura of completeness and wholeness which is representative of lives that have been lived successfully and purposefully.

Older adults face many varied social demands. Probably the most difficult of all of life's adjustments is that of becoming dependent on the children who have depended on their parents for so many years. The second most difficult adjustment is learning to adapt to the death of one's spouse and loving life partner. Special attention should be given to the social needs of older adults: to be noticed, appreciated, and included in ongoing activities wherever possible.

Spiritually

With their occupational pursuits behind them, many older adults find that they have more time and opportunity to give themselves to prayer, Bible reading, and Christian service than they had in earlier days. In the context of Christian nurture, we must be sure to provide activities that help these people meet each challenge of life. They should not be excluded from the rest of the Christian body or made to feel that no longer do they have a significant contribution to make. Our programs should recognize the value of these spiritual warriors who have fought the good fight of faith successfully. We should utilize their talents, skills, and wisdom whenever possible. This effort will lend dignity to their station in life and bless the body of Christ in the process.

16 Circle the letter in front of each TRUE statement.
a The process of change and development which characterizes childhood and adolescence ends as one enters adulthood.
b By middle adulthood one has achieved many of his earlier objectives; therefore, he is required to make a number of adjustments.
c As one enters the adult phase of life, he tends to develop a new, more mature relationship with his parents and with others who share common goals and interests.
d One of the characteristics of middle adulthood is a concern for others, which is often expressed through nurturing and teaching them.
e It is rather uncommon for one who has reached middle adulthood and raised a family successfully to experience vocational or marital problems.
f Christian nurturing classes should avoid topics related to marriage and partner adjustment.
g Christian nurturing classes should be conducted to help prepare adults for involvement in Christian service.
h The church should sponsor ministries that will help meet the social needs of older adults.
i Because older adults have passed the peak of their physical strength, they have little to offer the church that is useful.
j Adults are too old to receive Christ as their personal Savior.
k Adults need to be reminded to recognize and establish spiritual priorities.

Conclusion

Christian nurture is concerned about what is happening to people—individuals. While we often teach people in group settings, our concern is the wholeness of each person. Our concern is not that people have some knowledge of the Bible, but that they experience total life transformation into the likeness of Jesus Christ. We are concerned about the total person. Therefore, we need a good understanding of the individual, his growth and development characteristics, how he is similar to most other people of his age group, and how he differs from them.

Through Christian nurture we seek to encourage the growth and development of each Christian's new life. The more we know about the nature of that life and about the nature of the individual, the more effective will be our efforts to help him grow and develop. Learning should be planned to meet the needs of growing and developing learners.

self-test

1 Match each description of the characteristics of learners (left) with the appropriate period during which it occurs (right).

....**a** Boys develop physically during this stage as girls did a bit earlier, reason and judgment are developing to more sophisticated levels, home ties are weakening, dating is common

....**b** During this stage the heart develops more slowly than the rest of the body, person tires easily, has longer attention span, is beginning to read and write, likes Bible stories, and is developing a conscience

....**c** Bodies are nearly at the fully developed level, attention is on skills, interests concern one's vocation, the person wants to solve problems for himself, is reaching sexual maturity, has developing sense of loyalty

....**d** This stage is characterized by the attempt to find a marriage partner, establish a home, rear children, period of peak physical strength, period of unlimited mental capacity, time for seeking relationships in community and church

....**e** Time when one reflects on the past, wisdom graces this period of life, the person often projects an aura of wholeness and completeness

....**f** One here can't perform skilled mechanical functions, has the desire to touch everything, has a limited attention span and a vivid imagination, can memorize simple Bible verses

1) Early childhood
2) Middle childhood
3) Later childhood
4) Early adolescence
5) Middle adolescence
6) Later adolescence
7) Early adulthood
8) Middle adulthood
9) Later adulthood

....**g** Girls in this stage nearly reach adult height, it is the period when puberty is reached, the time when an awareness of self concept comes, one begins to have spiritual doubts

....**h** Period when many of a person's earlier objectives have been reached, his intellectual powers are devoted to production, it is the period of life for achievement, he develops a sense of caring for others, time of active involvement

....**i** The person has boundless energy, a healthy appetite, tends to be careless about grooming, is inquisitive mentally, observes accurately and reasons logically, likes to collect things, is quick to argue but doesn't hold grudges, boys and girls tend to be segregated into their own groups, they are hero worshipers and generally "ready for salvation"

2-10 In the following exercise, choose a word or words from the list below that either complete(s) the meaning or supplies the missing information.

will	heredity	abilities
intelligence	conduct	personality
imbalance	spiritual	nurtured
Christ-life	automatic	choices
whole	temporal	nonphysical
values	culture	environment

2 Human beings grow and develop physically, intellectually, emotionally, socially, and spiritually. Growth in the .... areas can continue until either death, senility, or physical deterioration disrupts the capacity for growth.

3 To be properly developed in each above-mentioned areas of life is to be ....

4 Christians place high priority on .... growth, because the .... is eternal; whereas, the other areas of human life are ....

5 Wholesome growth is not .... ; it must be encouraged and ....

6 .... exists when a person fails to develop properly in one or more of the basic areas of life.

7 .... is a comprehensive term which refers to the total of what a person is, including his thoughts, actions, attitudes, traits, temperament, and character.

8 One of the factors which affects human personality, the capacity one inherits from his parents, is called .... It seems to determine within rough limits a person's mental .... is one natural ability in which people vary greatly.

9 .... (our surroundings) also affects one's personality development. .... is also a part of one's environment. Each culture has its own .... and teaches .... based on them.

10 One's .... also affects his personality develoment. This component of personality is demonstrated in one's ability to make ....

answers to study questions

9 a)
d)
f)
h)
j)

1 a True.
b True.
c True.
d False.
e False.
f True.

10 Your answer. I've noted that quite often children I've observed in this age bracket are not well-coordinated physically as they play and color or draw. They wiggle and move considerably. They have limited vocabularies, but they often act out with gestures and facial expressions what they want to say. They tell stories very animatedly and employ graphic word pictures. They are very trusting and loving.

2 b) Later childhood.

11 a 1) Agree.
b 2) Disagree.
c 1) Agree.
d 2) Disagree.
e 2) Disagree.
f 1) Agree.
g 1) Agree.

3 c) Early adulthood.

12 Your answer. I've noticed that one could expect to see more of a balance between physical and nonphysical activities in play. You would tend to see a grouping of boys and girls playing together. You might also hear words being used incorrectly or mispronounced as the children tell stories or relate experiences. It would not be at all uncommon to hear one child say to another "That's not nice," or "You'd better not do that." Nor would it be odd to see the children in tears over some supposed injustice. In a learning situation, such as a Bible class, you would find the children to be eager learners, warm and receptive to the truth, and responsive to an appeal to accept Christ as their personal Savior.

4 a) Later adulthood.

13 **a** 1) Agree.
b 1) Agree.
c 2) Disagree.
d 1) Agree.
e 1) Agree.
f 1) Agree.
g 2) Disagree.

5 a) Early childhood.

14 Your answer. You would probably observe that children at this level display greater skill in the games they play than younger children. They would give evidence of unlimited energy, playing with all their hearts. You would find them enthralled by lab experiments, field trips, and guided study projects. You might overhear them making personal applications of spiritual truths or responding well to teaching on the responsibilities of Christians. Behind seemingly unemotional facades you undoubtedly would find sensitive youngsters who wanted attention, approval, and direction—even though they seem to be accepted by their peers and well adapted on the outside. You would also find a tendency for the girls and boys to segregate themselves in their own groups.

6 b) Early adolescence.

15 a 1) Appropriate.
   b 2) Not appropriate.
   c 1) Appropriate.
   d 2) Not appropriate.
   e 1) Appropriate.
   f 1) Appropriate.
   g 2) Not appropriate.
   h 1) Appropriate.
   i 1) Appropriate.
   j 2) Not appropriate.

7 c) Later adolescence.

16 a False.
   b True.
   c True.
   d True.
   e False.
   f False.
   g True.
   h True.
   i False.
   j False.
   k True.

8 a True.
   b False.
   c False.
   d True.
   e True.
   f False.

LESSON 6

Like Teacher - Like Learner

Maria was particularly excited one evening when Juan came home from his fields. That day Manuel had spoken his first word! Juan, realizing the significance of the event, was happy, too. It was amazing to see how quickly Manuel learned other words and their meanings. Encouraged by his parents, Manuel learned to identify objects, people, and places with their correct names. Soon he demonstrated the ability to arrange words into simple sentences. During this exciting period of growth Juan and Maria were often surprised to hear Manuel repeat words and expressions that were common to them. Before long Juan and Maria found that their little boy spent many of his waking hours in communication. He had the ability to express his ideas and carry on a conversation about a surprising number of things, especially those which interested him.

"Nothing unusual about that," you say? True enough, it is normal for children to develop the skills of talking during this period of their lives. But what is significant is that Manuel is growing up speaking the same language that the rest of the family speaks, rather than a different language. He is also learning to eat the same foods they enjoy and to act in ways that are typical of their area of the world. Why? The most reasonable explanation for this is the influence of his parents, because by this association his attitudes, feelings, and behaviors are formed.

Jesus said, "But everyone who is fully trained will be like his teacher" (Luke 6:40). This means that the learner is affected to a

162

$$t = t_0 \sqrt{1 - \frac{v^2}{c^2}}$$

great degree by the example of his teachers. Informal nurturing, then, has a vital role to play in developing Christian growth. In this lesson you will study more about the informal pattern of Christian nurture. You will be taught the value of learning through interacting and identifying with others. You will also discover who are the significnt models in Christian nurture.

lesson outline

Learning the Wholeness of Faith
Strategy of Socialization
Building Modeling Relationships
Appropriate Models Identified

lesson objectives

When you finish this lesson you should be able to:

- List reasons for teaching biblical facts as the basis of faith.

- Explain the relationship between socialization and Christian nurture.

- Discuss modeling relationships in Christian nurture.

- Identify those who are models in Christian nurture.

learning activities

1. Look up the meanings of any key words you do not understand.

2. Work through the lesson development as usual. As you do the study questions, be sure to write your own responses before you look ahead to the answers we have given. Take the self-test when you have finished and check your answers.

key words

affinity	context	intimidating
assumption	discrepancy	mutuality
commonalty	domineering	projects (verb)
competency	intensifies	socialization
compliance	internalization	voluntary
consistency		

lesson development

LEARNING THE WHOLENESS OF FAITH

Objective 1. *Choose statements which correctly identify how we learn the wholeness of faith.*

Do you remember how your Christian life began? Did you not believe the gospel, accept the offer of salvation, and commit your life to Christ? Of course you did. All of us began by making such a response to the gospel through faith. Because of this we experienced the new birth, which is the gateway to spiritual life. We have found that as we grow spiritually, we become more and more like Christ. Thus, our relationship with Him increasingly develops and matures so that we reflect His nature, character, and values, which are expressed through our living. That initial *faith response* to the gospel has led us to a life based on faith, a new quality of life that is characterized by wholeness in Jesus Christ. This wholeness that emerges out of our living faith may be referred to as the wholeness

164

of faith. But how do we learn wholeness through faith? Of what is it composed? How do we learn to live a Christ-like life?

Careful examination reveals that faith which brings wholeness is composed of both knowledge and life (faith applied to everyday life situations). God has spoken His message to us as truth that can be either accepted or rejected. This truth, which reveals both the nature and character of God and His purpose for man, has been recorded, preserved, and passed down to us as the Scriptures. Biblical truth is the source of knowledge that causes faith to grow and mature.

Some biblical truth is composed of *statements of fact*. For example, in the Ten Commandments we see something of what God is like, what He expected of His people, and the results of disobedience. Some truth takes the form of *concepts*, which are general ideas drawn from a number of experiences with things that are related (for example, oranges, bananas, and apples are called fruit). We learn the concept of holiness by many careful rules God gave in the Levitical law to separate nonsacred things from those that are holy. And finally, some truth appears as *principles* to be applied to life. For instance, the command to love God with our total being is a principle which governs our relationship with God primarily, but in practical application this principle should be the basis of our relationship with others. *Facts, concepts*, and *principles*, then, are the basis for a knowledge based on faith. It is necessary to have this knowledge in order to develop to wholeness in Jesus Christ. Without this knowledge we cannot know how to live the life of faith that truly pleases God.

In addition to the written witness, God revealed Himself in living form in the person of Jesus Christ. John says "The Word became flesh and lived for a while among us. We have seen His glory . . . " (John 1:14). Moreover, Peter states that he was an eyewitness of Christ's majesty, honor and glory (2 Peter 1:16-18) and asserts that in coming to earth he left us an example to follow in His steps (1 Peter 2:20-25). He demonstrated to us how to live life to the fullest, how to be everything God intends us to be. His life is an example of the life of faith that pleases God fully. (Obedience, submission, willingness to do the Father's will, and His commitment to love wholly those whom the Father willed to save, in spite of their hostility to Him.)

By studying this course you may have already discovered that learning involves more than merely acquiring facts and information. Understanding the information, integrating it into our beliefs, and changing our behavior accordingly are also important.

In Lessons 1 and 2 you were taught the importance of God's Word in spiritual growth. In Lesson 3 you learned of the importance of disciplemaking and modeling in spiritual growth. Both biblical knowledge and examples of how this knowledge can be applied practically in the Christian life are helpful in nurturing Christian growth.

We concluded Unit 1 by observing that Christian nurture requires both informal and formal patterns. Biblical information—facts, concepts, and principles—can be taught through formal patterns which involve classroom-type teaching-learning activities. But understanding values and appropriate Christian behaviors are communicated through intimate interactions and the personal identification of learners with others. Learning wholeness that is based on faith requires the formal, systematic study of God's Word and the informal, often unstructured, nurturing that occurs as one relates on a very personal level with and imitates his models.

1 Circle the letter preceding each TRUE statement.
a Faith's wholeness is learned primarily by attending specialized classes.
b Both biblical knowledge and appropriate examples of the Christian life are needed for a balanced program of Christian nurture.
c Christian nurture requires both informal and formal patterns.
d The only thing one needs to do to nurture faith's wholeness is teach biblical truth.
e Biblical knowledge can be taught through formal types of learning activities.
f Understanding, values, and behavior are communicated through informal nurturing techniques.

Because both informal and formal patterns of Christian nurture are essential, we will consider more carefully the informal pattern in this lesson. Then, in Lesson 7 we will focus our attention on practical matters that concern teaching God's Word in the formal pattern.

STRATEGY OF SOCIALIZATION

Socialization Defined

Objective 2. *Select a statement which defines the meaning of socialization.*

I once heard an unschooled man say, "Some things are better 'caught' than 'taught'." He was speaking about what the professional might call *socialization*. Before we can accept *socialization* as a strategy for Christian nurture, we need to understand the meaning of the term.

Socialization is the process of integrating a person into a given social context—preparing him to function meaningfully within a particular association or grouping of people. It entails developing a meaningful understanding of the society and social order in which one lives. It is the process of learning language, norms, values, attitudes, and proper behavior as perceived by a given group of people. Socialization refers to learning, not in the traditional, formal sense of schooling, but in the sense of absorbing the affects of our environment.

2 Circle the letter preceding the statement which most accurately defines the term *socialization*, based on the foregoing discussion. Socialization refers to
a) the process of teaching information in a formal schooling pattern.
b) developing a meaningful understanding of one's society in order to function competently in a given social context.
c) adapting the Christian gospel to fit the social values of a given people.

167

Socialization Illustrated

Objective **3.** *Cite practical examples of the processes of socialization.*

How do you eat food? Do you use a fork or a spoon? Maybe you use chopsticks, or possibly you eat with your fingers. The way you eat was learned through socialization. If you are accustomed to eating in a particular way, you may find other ways uncomfortable and unnatural. You learned the proper way to eat food in your culture by watching others and by doing what you saw them do. You may have been quite surprised to discover that some people in the world eat differently than you do.

This illustration of eating is an example of a behavior which is highly cultural in practice. What is socially acceptable in one culture may be considered unacceptable, impolite, or even rude in another. Values are learned by socialization. You may have observed that different cultural groups live and act in different ways. They hold different values. Children born in one group grow up knowing the ways and wisdom of their group, while those born in another group grow up knowing, valuing, and acting differently. The reason for these differences is that each has learned the ways of his culture through socialization.

How did you learn to speak your native tongue? Perhaps you can't tell me; you may feel that you have always known how to speak your language. Perhaps you are more comfortable using it than any you may have learned since. While you may feel as though you have always known your native language, we understand that indeed you did learn it. What if, as soon as you were born, you had been taken to live in another area of the world where a different language is used? You would undoubtedly have grown up knowing that language instead of the one you now use, for we learn language through the process of socialization.

3 List in your notebook two or three examples of the processes of socialization.

Socialization Explained

Objective 4. *Select statements which correctly explain socialization.*

Socialization takes place in the context of shared experiences in a real-life setting. We develop behavior in ways that are in keeping with our beliefs and values. These actions are observed by those near us and become the basis of their learning through socialization. Because of the nature of the relationship, learning through socialization is often unorganized, unstructured and not systematically planned. It simply occurs as the life setting provides the opportunities.

Learning through socialization is instruction by modeling. People learn by what they see demonstrated, as we have seen in our consideration of the master-apprentice relationship. The way of life and the understanding and values which support a given life style are communicated in such a way that they are clearly seen and understood by those who are members of that society. As a learner practices what he learns from the social models, he desires to experience the same quality of life.

Developing intimate relationships with others is another essential part of socialization. An individual usually knows someone after whom he wishes to pattern his behavior. This other person becomes a model for the learner. Quite frequently, an affinity develops between the model and the pupil which we call *mutuality*, which is expressed in caring for each other, trust, recognition of the other's worth and value, and feelings of interdependence.

Likewise, socialization requires opportunities for the learner to imitate the model. Life provides many such opportunities. Since most effective modeling takes place in real-life settings, the imitating needs to occur in real-life experiences, too. The learner attempts to repeat what he has observed the model do. His effort at doing what he has seen the model do is a learning response. As the learner acts for himself, he looks to the model for signals of approval or disapproval of his response.

4 From each of the preceding four paragraphs, choose the statement which explains best what is essential to learning in socialization. Then write each of these in the following spaces.

a ....

b ....

c ....

d ....

Socialization Applied

Objective **5**. *Select statements which show the relationship between socialization and Christian nurture.*

One way we learn the Christ-life is through the process of socialization. We learn to live the abundant new life given by Jesus in the same way we learned the customs and language of our culture. The values, attitudes, motives, conscience, and behaviors appropriate to the Christ-life are absorbed through meaningful, intimate relationships with people whose lives model the Christ-life.

The learning process goal is to nurture the new life Jesus gives. It seeks to help that life develop to maturity and to be expressed in all areas of our lives. This goal is facilitated through the socialization process. The discipling pattern Jesus used when he taught the Twelve is needed in the Christian nurturing ministry today.

We must recognize the powerful influence which exists in the modeling interactions between the teacher and the learner, and we must encourage these relationships. You can help people mature spiritually by entering into significant, intimate relationships with them, even as Thessalonian believers did (1 Thessalonians 1:7).

5 Locate and read the following verses in your Bible: 1 Corinthians 11:1; Ephesians 5:1; Philippians 3:17; 1 Thessalonians 1:6; and Hebrews 6:12. Observe carefully how the writer emphasizes the need to follow godly examples and imitate patterns of behavior which are appropriate to the Christian life. Think seriously about the meanings of these verses and how they may be applied to your own life. Write your observations and thought in your notebook.

6 Circle the letter preceding each TRUE statement.
a We learn to live the Christ life through the process of socialization.
b While socialization is useful in learning one's customs, it is inappropriate for nurturing spiritual growth.
c Intimate relations with other people are powerful factors in the Christian nurturing ministry.
d The New Testament encourages believers to imitate godly models.
e Jesus avoided using the socialization process when discipling the Twelve, choosing to use spiritual means.

BUILDING MODELING RELATIONSHIPS

Objective 6. *Select statements which explain how to build modeling relationships.*

When we experience the new birth, the life of Jesus is not fully developed in us. The task of those involved in the Christian nurturing ministry is to cultivate this new life toward spiritual maturity. The end of this process will be development into the likeness of Jesus — the maturing of His life within us. This likeness is communicated through modeling relationships.

171

One of our characteristics is to strive for competency—to be adequate, both in our own opinion and in the opinion of others. In some societies, much emphasis is placed on proving one's competency as a student. In other societies, one might be driven to prove his competency as an athlete, a breadwinner, parent, neighbor, or citizen. Whether you have been aware of it or not, Christians are to be competent as witnesses and effective servants of Jesus Christ. Paul, for example, explains his efforts to be competent as a soldier of the cross (1 Corinthians 9:24-27). This example shows how the desire for competency reaches into the realm of spiritual things. In the process of striving for competency we often seek out those whom we perceive to be competent and mature and attempt to imitate them—to adapt their traits, values, and character.

You may have experienced this in your own life. Perhaps you know someone who possesses a skill which you value. You may wish you could be like that person. Have you heard a musician whom you consider to be very good and felt that you would like to be able to play an instrument as that person does? You may have tried to develop the techniques and style of that person. In a certain way, this is a modeling relationship. We also seek to find people whose lives seem ideal and desirable to us. Then we seek to emulate their lives and become like them. Modeling is a primary means of communicating likeness.

A modeling relationship is a resourceful relationship. The more mature person provides support and help for the one who is less mature. It is a helping relationship. The purpose of such a relationship is to uphold the weaker or less mature person until he develops competency. In terms of the Christian life, this means that the teacher gives supportive assistance until the learner develops spiritual stature and begins to reflect the likeness of Christ.

The modeling relationship, however, is not a domineering relationship. The model should not "smother" his disciple. He should not decide all the issues for him. In fact, no obligations should exist in the modeling relationship which hinder growth and development. The learner should not perceive the relationship as either threatening or intimidating. Instead, he should respect his model highly and strive to be like him, because he demonstrates true qualities of Christlikeness. The learner will also see how his model responds to various issues of life and how the likeness of Christ radiates from him under all kinds of situations, and how his values and behavior are consistent with the nature of the Christ life. On this basis the learner should seek to become like him. It is a voluntary relationship, which is based on the exemplary life the model lives and the disciple perceives. The model responds to the biblical commands to nurture the spiritual life of the less mature; the disciple responds because of his own needs for advice, instruction, encouragement, and intimate fellowship.

In building the modeling relationship, we must strive for the kind of response in learners that will be truly Christ-exalting and that will lead to a deeper commitment to Him and His work. There are, in fact, various levels of response to the modeling relationship. The lowest level, called *compliance*, is that in which learners do the Lord's work simply because we ask them to. They simply comply in order to be cooperative and to be accepted by us and our immediate Christian group. They do what is asked without personal commitment. Then there is a second level of response referred to as *identification*. Because of their great respect for the leader and their own desire to be like him, learners perform the work without any particular commitment to it. While *identification* is motivated out of sincere admiration for the model and their desire to please him, there is not true dedication to the work. Finally, the highest level of response is that in which learners claim the model's work and Christian goals as their own. This is called *internalization*. The purpose of the work is integrated into their own value system. Learners perceive the Lord's work as an expression of their love to God and an opportunity to exercise their own gifts and commitments. They delight in following their model, but in so doing they reach their own Christian goals as they fulfill the larger calling to do the Master's work. When learners respond in this latter way, we can rejoice in the fruit that has resulted from the modeling relationship.

In summary, we can say that the goal of the modeling relationship is much more "being" than "doing." It involves what the learner *is,* more than what he *does.* The desired result of the modeling relationship is for the disciple to "become," not just "act," like the model.

In the Christian nurturing ministry we enter into disciplining relationships with people—opening our lives for them to observe and imitate. This relationship may require us to do many of the following with learners: make applications of the Word to life situations, consider Christian privileges and responsibilities, endeavor to know and do God's will. Above all, we must set a pattern in conversation, behavior, the use of time, talents, finances, and relationships that demonstrate the centrality of Christ in our own life. To prepare yourself for this role, therefore, you need to "be" the kind of person others will desire to pattern themselves after, to give living expression to the life of Christ in such a degree of maturity that others will recognize that by imitating you their own spiritual life will be nurtured toward wholeness. This means that you, too, will seek to be increasingly like Christ.

The awesomeness of the role of a model should be humbling. The fact that others seek to become like you should not cause you to become proud. The responsibility of nurturing the spiritual life of growing Christians is great, and it is for this reason James warned that Christian teachers will be judged more severely (James 3:1).

7 In the following exercises, match the appropriate level of response (right) indicated for each of the following descriptive statements (left).

....**a** "Dieter never seems to have his heart in what he does. He simply carries out our requests."

....**b** "Because of great admiration for his teacher, Raymond carries out the task associated with his job; however, he doesn't have any real commitment to the Lord's work."

....**c** "Mona seems to be a reflection of her teacher. She is committed to

1) Internalization
2) Identification
3) Compliance

the tasks the teacher has adopted as her own, for she recognizes that it is the Lord's work. She is very happy in her work. As she does the tasks assigned by her model, she is reaching her own personal goals as well. This brings her a deep sense of satisfaction."

....d "The one said, 'I'll go,' but he didn't. Later, however, he repented and went."

....e "During Jesus' ministry, His disciples willingly did His bidding; however, they neither understood nor appreciated His long-term work or the cost involved."

8 Circle the letter preceding each TRUE statement.

a In our efforts to grow and mature spritually, we will find help by seeking to establish relationships with those whose lives reflect true Christlikeness.

b Modeling relationships by their very nature are intended to be permanent.

c The modeling relationship exists for the purpose of bringing together the support and help of more mature people for the benefit of those who are less mature.

d The modeling relationship is not built on the assumption that the model should dominate the relationship; rather, it is constructed so that the learner can have opportunity to imitate the behaviors he has seen demonstrated by the model.

e The learner has as his primary goal "to act" like his model, for the important issue is acting not being.

f As one matures in his Christian experience, he should endeavor to be the kind of person people will want to pattern their lives after. His life should demonstrate Christlikeness so that people can see that it is both possible and practical to develop toward true Christian wholeness.

Togetherness and Likeness

Objective 7. *Choose statements which identify four essential factors of modeling relationships.*

How do we get to know someone well enough to develop likeness to him? Or, how do we enter into relationships in such a way that the other person will get to know us well enough to desire to become truly like us?

Modeling relationships require being together with someone frequently in a variety of situations over a long period of time. This togetherness must be developed in a real-life setting. In this developing relationship, the inner life of the model is opened to the learner. The model must exhibit consistency between the ideals of spiritual maturity and his own behavior so that there is no discrepancy between what he "preaches" and what he "practices." The learner should have ample opportunity, also, to imitate what he observes. All of these foregoing essentials may be observed from what you have previously studied in this lesson. Perhaps we may summarize these observations into four essential factors of modeling relationships: 1) interaction, 2) intimacy, 3) identification, and 4) imitating.

Interaction refers to the impact of one life upon another. Wherever lives intersect there is interaction. As your life touches that of someone else, you interact together. Interaction implies that some form of communication exchange has taken place between you, and it implies that each of you has had an effect on the life of the other. Interaction can be thought of as the first step in the development of interpersonal relationships. Interaction begins on a surface or shallow level, but over a period of time it deepens and intensifies. Interaction engages us in a movement process which takes us from ourselves or from self-centeredness toward another's orientation and viewpoint of life. It is as we interact with others that we learn to value their personhood. As we relate together we develop an awareness of the worth and dignity of the other person, and we tend to clarify our own sense of self-worth as well.

Relationships which are characterized by *interaction* often tend to deepen toward intimacy. *Intimacy* implies closeness and familiarity. It is marked by deep emotional bonds of warm friendship which develop through association. Intimacy suggests informality and warmth which is personal and private between persons who have developed close relationships. Their association is such that each feels secure and at liberty to reveal his innermost thoughts to the other and finds satisfaction and fulfillment in knowing the other person in this familiar way. Modeling relationships are most effective when they are intimate relationships. It is in this in-depth knowing of another person that one observes the model's true self, sees in him what he perceives to be competency, and desires to be like him.

In the context of Christian community, intimacy naturally results from the commonalty of shared life. Two people who are living the Christ-life possess something in common that binds them strongly together; they belong to each other but as different members of one body. This mutuality in Jesus Christ is the basis for spiritual love, the deepest and highest expression of intimacy.

Identification implies projecting oneself into the life of someone else. It means that we see in another person traits and characteristics which we feel are desirable. Identification implies a person becoming emotionally attached to another person in such a way that he believes himself to be like that person in vital ways. Identification often results in a vicarious sharing of experiences. It means to relate so closely with another that you strive to be like that person. I once knew a small boy who identified himself so much with a sports star that he asked his mother to call him by the star's name.

Imitating involves relating so closely to another person that you endeavor to become what he is. It is the attempt to resemble another person. It is more, however, than merely striving to act as the other person acts or to do what he does. It involves striving to be what that person is. It means being influenced so fully by another person that you reflect his characteristics, approach to life, including his thinking and feeling, as well as his behavior. You do what he does, not to please him, but to please yourself in your desire to be like him. Imitating results in internalizing the values and life style of another person to the extent you begin to experience them as your own values and life-style. Togetherness builds likeness. Interpersonal relationships, therefore, develop from interaction to intimacy to identification to imitating.

In the Christian nurturing ministry, where the goal is to help others develop into Christlikeness, this concept finds particular application. The more mature Christian's most intense desire should be to allow the life of Christ within him to develop and grow until he identifies completely with Jesus and His life becomes a living expression through his own life. In this way others will see the nature of Christ expressed in him. The goal of the body of Christ should be to embody the life of Christ with expressions of the Christ-life which are so powerful that others will want to identify deeply with our Lord. Since you are a part of that body, as all Christians are, your life becomes a living expression of the Christ-life—a model for others to imitate. As they imitate you, they begin to develop and grow toward Christlikeness. What a challenging, yet wonderful, responsibility and privilege!

9 Circle the letters before the following statements which are TRUE.
a In modeling relationships one person becomes like the other.
b Interaction is the most in-depth level of interpersonal relationships.
c Interaction refers to the impact of one life upon another.
d Deep emotional bonds characterize intimacy.
e Intimacy implies sheltering oneself from another person.
f Identification in the context of modeling, means finding one's own self-identity apart from human relationships.
g In identification one projects himself into the life of another person.
h In imitating one relates so closely with another person that he becomes what the other person is.
i Imitating implies that one assumes the behavior of someone else.
j Modeling concepts are difficult to apply in the Christian nurturing ministry.

APPROPRIATE MODELS IDENTIFIED

Objective 8. *Select statements which identify appropriate models of the Christian life.*

Modeling the Christ-life is a powerful means of communication, which nurtures spiritual growth toward Christlikeness. To whom can new converts look for a meaningful modeling relationship? Who are the appropriate models of the Christ-life?

Parents are involved in modeling relationships with their children. Bonds between tender, impressionable children and their parents naturally exist. All of the essential factors necessary for modeling relationships should be present in normal family relationships— closeness, the opportunity to observe, meaningful involvement together, and mutual love. These characteristics should be present in the relationship between parents and children.

The Bible recognizes that this natural modeling relationship should exist between parents and their children. In fact, under the Law God commanded parents to be appropriate models by their obedience to His statutes, judgments, and ordinances.

10 Read Deuteronomy 6:1-9 carefully. After you have read these verses and meditated on their significance, write in your notebook the answers to the questions which follow.
a What do you think about the message of the Deuteronomy passage?
b To whom was this passage addressed?
c List the specific instructions given in verses 5-9.
d What did these specific commands mean to those who originally received them?
e Compare Ephesians 5:1 with Deuteronomy 6:1-9 and explain why these instructions were given.

179

11 Read Judges 2:10-15 and then circle the letter of the best completion to the following question, based upon this Scripture reference. The generation of Israel which arose not knowing the Lord and His mighty acts represents primarily

a) Israel's failure to integrate the culture of the land properly in her own value system.
b) Israel's desire to be liberal in her interpretation of God's laws.
c) failure in the home, where spiritual values were to have been transmitted.
d) a breakdown of the public education system, which is the institution responsible for the transmission of spiritual and moral values.

I hope you understand better, from the Deuteronomy passage and the preceding questions, why Moses instructed parents in the nation of Israel to live exemplary lives before their children. Parents were to love God totally—to be examples worthy of modeling. They were to keep God's commands in their hearts—to value spiritual things. They were to teach these to their children by giving priority to spiritual things in their family relationships. Their homes were to be centers of religious instruction. Christian parents, likewise, are commanded to be models of the Christ-life.

Another level of close association and interaction for an individual is generally a small group of significant friends. This group may include family members, neighbors, and friends of the family. Many of these people may naturally be appropriate models. You may think of persons with whom you maintain such a relationship. They could be models for you, if they are more mature spiritually than you, or, you may be a model for them, if they are not as mature spiritually as you are.

You may have already discovered from your study of this course that God has designed some people in the church to serve specifically as teachers. All of the passages which deal with the gift ministries make particular reference to teachers. People in the church who serve as teachers have a particular obligation to maintain lives worthy of imitating. Teachers have a scriptural duty to live lives which teach the truths of the Word through their own behaviors, values, life-styles, and attitudes (1 Timothy 4:12).

In a very real sense, because of the nature of the Christian church, every believer should be a model for others to imitate. Paul told the Christians at Corinth that they were like living epistles read by everyone around them (2 Corinthians 3:1-3). He said that it was as though God's Word had been written in their hearts. This means that their lives were to be living expressions of Christlikeness that everyone could see. Because of the intimate nature of the body of Christ, modeling relationships naturally exist. In some cases, others may see in you the quality of spiritual vitality they desire to experience and seek to be like you without your awareness of their desire. More importantly, however, you should seek consciously to develop relationships at the in-depth level that fosters intimacy, identification, and imitating.

12 Circle the letter preceding each TRUE statement.

a Family relationships ideally contain the essential factors of modeling relationships.

b Since Christians are to keep their eyes on Jesus, the example they set is not all that important to others.

c The Bible commands parents to model spiritual reality for their children.

d Significant friends can be appropriate models to be imitated.

e Teachers in the church should give more concern to what they say than how they live.

f Teachers in the church have a particular responsibility to maintain lives worthy of imitating

g All Christians should live lives which are expressions of Christlikeness for everyone to see.

I have new appreciation for the statement of Jesus, "Everyone who is fully trained will be like his teacher." Christian nurturing, in its work of helping people mature toward Christlikeness, accomplishes its task of communicating life through the socialization process. This includes building modeling relationships and leads to a like teacher—like learner result. The interpersonal relationships which exist among members of the body of Christ are appropriate means of modeling the reality which nurture spiritual growth.

self-test

Circle the letter in front of the correct answer for each of the following questions.

1 Our primary reasons for teaching biblical facts as the basis of faith are indicated by all of the following except one. Which reason is NOT mentioned in this lesson?

a) Biblical facts are the foundation for faith's knowledge.

b) Biblical facts are the source of knowledge that causes faith to grow.

c) Biblical facts have been presented as statements of fact, some as concepts, and some as principles.

d) Biblical facts have all been presented through the impersonal means of recorded revelation.

2 According to the lesson, one teaches biblical facts as the basis of faith because
a) there is no alternative method by which one can impart moral and ethical values.
b) they are what God has communicated to us as truth that can be accepted or rejected.
c) of the value attached to them by the church.
d) this is the precedent of teaching set by the apostles.

3 Facts of Bible knowledge and appropriate examples of Christian life are needed for a balanced program of Christian nurture. These are taught most effectively by
a) formal and informal patterns.
b) the learner himself.
c) church educational programs.
d) social and cultural influence.

4 One reason, according to this lesson, why we use *socialization* as a strategy for Christian nurture is that
a) it is the easiest method to teach others and it requires no formal structures.
b) this means offers the most rapid results for the amount of effort expended.
c) it is the most natural thing for all people to do well, that is, model the Christ-life.
d) appropriate values, attitudes, motives, and behaviors of the Christ-life are absorbed through meaningful relationsips with others who model it.

5 All of the following but one are true concerning socialization. Which statement is NOT true?
a) We learn to live the Christ-life through the process of socialization.
b) The New Testament encourages believers to imitate godly models.
c) While socialization is useful in learning one's customs, it is not appropriate for nurturing spiritual growth.
d) Jesus employed the socialization process when He discipled the Twelve.

6 According to your lesson, modeling relationships are useful in Christian nurture because people naturally strive for competency and seek to imitate competent persons; therefore, one
a) feels that it is natural to model his spiritual life after one who demonstrates Christlikeness.
b) believes that the modeling relationship permits him to develop naturally in his daily life experiences.
c) tends to believe that by adopting a spiritual model and imitating his behavior, he will eliminate many of the difficult experiences of spiritual development.
d) follows models for all of the foregoing reasons stated in a), b), and c).
e) develops a modeling relationship because of the things mentioned in a) and b) above.

7 Modeling relationships are a productive and efficient method for transmitting values and strategies for spiritual development. Which one of the following statements is NOT a reason for or a goal of these relationships?
a) Modeling relationships are resourceful: the strong help the weak, giving supportive assistance to them until they develop spiritual competency.
b) The goal of the modeling relationship is for the model to strive to live a Christ-exalting life that will lead learners to a deeper commitment to Christ and His work.
c) The model must control the relationship totally until the learner has demonstrated full Christian maturity and competency in all spiritual matters.
d) The modeling relationship is a voluntary one; it is based on the life the model lives and the learner perceives.

8 If the modeling relationship is to be successful, learners must
a) be able to act precisely like the models they have adopted.
b) maintain this relationship permanently and surrender their initiative to act to their models.
c) concentrate more on activities than on any other aspect of their lives.
d) have the opportunity to apply what they have learned, demonstrating the behaviors they have observed in their models.

9 The lesson discussed four essential ingredients for the development of effective modeling relationships. The order in which these relationships develop was:
a) imitating, identification, intimacy, and interaction.
b) interaction, intimacy, identification, and imitating.
c) identification, interaction, intimacy, and imitating.
d) intimacy, interaction, imitating, and identification.

10 Appropriate models which one should strive to imitate, according to the lesson, include
a) the great evangelists, pastors, apostles of the past, and Bible heroes.
b) those who keep themselves apart from society for spiritual development in secluded places.
c) significant friends, family members, teachers, and, in essence, all Christians.
d) the older generation of mature people which has conquered the forces of evil successfully.

answers to study questions

7 a 3) Compliance.
  b 2) Identification.
  c 1) Internalization.
  d 3) Compliance.
  e 2) Identification.

1 a False.
  b True.
  c True.
  d False.
  e True.
  f True.

8 a True.
  b False.
  c True.
  d True.
  e False.
  f True.

2 b) developing a meaningful understanding of one's society.

9 a True.
  b False.
  c True.
  d True.
  e False.
  f False.
  g True.
  h True.
  i True.
  j False.

3 Your answer. You might have listed, among other things, the following: which foods are to be eaten and which are not, behavior that is acceptable and that which is unacceptable, what are appropriate goals for life, which values are appropriate, and what social rules one is expected to follow.

10 a Your answer. It occurs to me that a loving God is speaking to His children to ensure that their future would be blessed as they maintain their relationship with Him.

b It was addressed to the parents in the nation of Israel.

c Love God totally, keep His commandments by living according to their dictates, teach them to your children, and, of course, this implies modeling as well.

d They perceived these commandments as solemn and binding responsibilities. Future blessing depended upon obedience to them.

e These instructions were given on a conditional basis and were intended to challenge Israel to follow the Lord closely and thereby enjoy His blessings, including long life and material blessings.

4 a Socialization takes place in the context of shared experiences in a real-life setting.

b Learning through socialization requires instruction by modeling.

c Developing intimate relationships with others is another essential part of socialization.

d Likewise, socialization requires opportunities for the learner to imitate the model.

11 c) failure in the home.

5 Your answer.

12 a True.
b False.
c True.
d True.
e False.
f True.
g True.

6 a True.
  b False.
  c True.
  d True.
  e False.

LESSON 7

Guiding the Learning Experience

Manuel enjoyed going to school and found the lessons to be fun. At first the tasks were quite simple: memorizing the alphabet, recognizing the printed letters, counting from 1 to 10, and spelling his name. Later the tasks became more difficult and he learned to read, spell, write and solve mathematical problems.

When Maria went to a parent-teacher conference, she found that Manuel was a good pupil and she could understand why. Miss Gonzales, Manuel's teacher, knew how to help children learn. She knew how to make learning experiences interesting, challenging, and effective.

Biblical information can be learned when a teacher guides the learning experience. In directing Bible study, teachers lead learners to investigate the Scriptures, to determine their implications, and to apply them to their own lives.

In this lesson, you will study the teaching task, what discovery Bible study involves, how to do inductive Bible study, and how to plan meaningful learning encounters.

lesson outline

The Teaching Task
Discovery Bible Study
Inductive Bible Study
Planning Learning Encounters

lesson objectives

When you finish this lesson you should be able to:

■ Define the teaching task.

■ Describe two approaches to discovery Bible study.

■ Describe how to plan a meaningful learning encounter.

191

learning activities

1. Review briefly the material you studied in Lesson 4, especially what is involved in the teaching task.

2. Study the opening paragraphs, outline, and objectives. Then work through the lesson development according to the usual procedure. After you have completed the lesson, take the self-test and check your answers.

3. Carefully review Unit 2 (Lessons 4-7), especially the lesson objectives and self-tests. Then complete the unit student report for Unit 2 and send it to your instructor.

key words

criteria	perspective
encounter	probing
heresy	valid
passive	warrant

lesson development

THE TEACHING TASK

In our last lesson we discussed wholeness based on faith. Wholeness, we saw, develops as we gain Bible knowledge, which includes many basic facts and deeper doctrinal truths. As food is to the physical body so is biblical content to spiritual life. In fact, it is the source of faith (Romans 10:17). We found that wholeness requires not only knowledge but also the application of this knowledge to every day life situations. As we grow in knowledge and apply it consistently, we develop a lifestyle that is characterized by faith.

What is the value of growing in faith? What difference does it make if we develop spiritually, gain stature in the faith, and know many biblical facts? Is this development an end in itself? By no means is this the goal of Christian maturity, for our lives are not lived in isolation. We are admonished to grow in grace (2 Peter 3:18), become workmen who correctly handle the word of truth (2 Timothy 2:15), and be prepared to give an answer to everyone who asks us to give the reason for the hope we have (1 Peter 3:15). We are saved to serve others in the body of Christ, especially those who are spiritual babes. Our own growing experiences and our knowledge of God's Word enable us to teach others and thus strengthen the body of Christ and make possible its extension.

In Lesson 6 we examined the *informal pattern* of Christian nurture. We saw that whereas much learning takes place informally in the home and neighborhood in the natural process (socialization), so in the spiritual realm we learn the Christ life by imitating the attitudes and behavior of more mature Christians. Finally, we discussed the importance of our own character development as a means of becoming the kind of persons that others will want to imitate.

Now we consider *formal patterns* of Christian nurturing. In this lesson you will study how to teach biblical truth through teaching-learning activities in the classroom setting.

The Teaching Task Defined

Objective 1. *Choose statements which identify correctly the teaching task and explain why learning involves change.*

We have seen that the teaching task is more than imparting information. It is more than telling or talking. Telling a story, stating

193

facts, describing events, or explaining information may not necessarily equal effective teaching. If no one learns, teaching is apparently ineffective. At this point we must analyze the problem. Has the teacher failed to communicate effectively because he has used poor teaching methods? Has he appealed to only one of the senses and failed to enhance his students' learning experiences by ignoring the seeing, hearing, and interacting opportunities that tend to enrich their learning experience? The saying "a salesman has not sold a product until the customer has made a purchase" is somewhat appropriate for the teaching-learning experience. If, for example, the learner doesn't learn effectively, then our teaching is ineffective or faulty. One doesn't just deliver a lecture or teach a lesson and assume that learning will occur automatically. Teaching and learning are so vitally intertwined that to be meaningful one cannot be effective unless the other is. Truth should not be dispensed in a tasteless way, and it cannot be imposed on a learner. He cannot be forced to learn. How, then, should the teaching task be done?

We should reemphasize our earlier point: that the learner must interact with the material and discover truth for himself if the learning experience is to be meaningful to him. No teacher can do that for the learner. However, truth can be discovered under the guidance and leadership of a teacher. Teachers, therefore, are guides in the process of learning. The teaching task is to facilitate learning, to help learners learn. The learner must integrate the new material he learns with what he has already learned. He must consider how it relates to him, apply it in his own life, and bring his life into harmony with the truth he discovers. This is why we say, "change is essential to learning." Thus, the teacher is a "change agent." When change is demonstrated in attitudes, values, and behavior, we know that learning has occurred.

Both the learner and the teacher play important roles in the teaching-learning process. The following chart shows each role and the relationship of each to the other.

194

TEACHING RESPONSIBILITIES	LEARNING RESPONSIBILITIES
Motivate interaction, stimulate curiosity, organize material	Interact with the material
Guide discovery, prescribe appropriate activities	Discover truth for one's self
Ask life-related questions, give examples which are life-related, pose life-related problems	Make personal applications of truth to one's own life
Support, suggest, correct, pray, and trust God	Bring one's life into harmony with truth

The teaching task, then, involves *creating* an environment in which learning can take place, *motivating* learning, and *guiding* discovery. Teaching involves *structuring opportunities* in which learning can occur. It includes *planning* activities which will enable the student to encounter and interact with the material and *designing* experiences which lead to change. To bring about the desired change, that is, to move learners from their present level to that desired by the teacher, the teacher must: 1) determine what the learners know (often this is accomplished by means of a pretest), 2) specify learning objectives, 3) prescribe learning activities that will lead to the fulfillment of the objectives, and 4) evaluate progress.

THE TEACHING TASK

1. Pretest
2. Specify objectives
3. Prescribe learning activities
4. Evaluate progress

195

1 Circle the letter preceding each statement which identifies correctly an aspect of the teaching task, based on the foregoing discussion.
a) Delivering a lecture
b) Guiding the learning process
c) Structuring opportunities for learning to occur
d) Telling learners what to do about a truth
e) Motivating learning
f) Planning activities to help learners change
g) Creating a learning environment
h) Talking about a subject
i) Facilitating learning
j) Stating factual information

2 From our discussion of the definition of the teaching task, we can make the following conclusions. Supply the missing word to complete the following summary of that teaching task.

a To facilitate the learning experience the teacher should

.... the process of learning.

b As related to biblical truth, the teacher's task is to help learners

.... God's truth and .... it to their lives.

3 Explain in your notebook why change is essential to learning.

If you as the teacher are to direct the learning experience effectively, you must understand the principle of discovery Bible study. You must also be able to guide learners in this method of study.

DISCOVERY BIBLE STUDY

Discovery Bible Study Defined

Objective 2. *Distinguish from a list of statements those that give true definitions of discovery Bible study.*

As you study further into methods that nurture Christian growth, it will be helpful for you to put yourself occasionally in the learner's role to see how learning experiences affect him. For example, would you rather be involved actively in learning situations, or do you prefer to receive passively what others prepare? As an active participant, you can enjoy the fruit of your own labor; as a passive recipient, you receive the benefit of someone else's labor. In the learning experience this means either that you do your own thinking or you have others think for you. You may have experienced, as I have, the satisfaction of personal accomplishment. If so, you will probably agree that few experiences are more rewarding.

Perhaps you have experienced an exciting moment when a new truth burst in on you. Before that moment you did not know it; after that moment, you could never forget it. You discovered truth! Nowhere is this experience more thrilling and enjoyable than in Bible study. Personal discovery of God's truth revealed in the Bible is a wonderful experience.

To discover truth means that you obtain for the first time insight into or knowledge of previously existing truth. It involves uncovering, exposing, disclosing, or bringing into light truth which you did not previously know. Discovery is not inventing or making up new information. The truth existed before, but for the first time you perceive or discover it. God's truth has always existed. It was recorded in the Bible. The Bible student's task is to discover God's truth, not invent it.

Discovery Bible study, then, is a method of study which leads the learner to study the Scriptures to uncover the truth God has revealed and how it applies to his own life. He approaches this study with the assumption that God's truth is to be obeyed and lived out in his own life. God's truth is more than facts to be known; when applied to his life, it is a living testimony to the dynamic power and vitality of the Christian life. The learner is thus actively involved in the processes of finding out what God has revealed, how this truth relates to him, and how he may apply it in his own life. In discovery Bible study the learner is personally involved in searching the Scriptures to learn what God is revealing. His intention is to respond obediently to Him. This is what the Christians at Berea did: they searched or examined the Scriptures so that they could respond appropriately to the truth (Acts 17:11).

In discovery Bible study, we are confronted first with our true spiritual needs (which are often different from our current nonspiritual interests and the things which concern our earthly goals, that is, our life needs). Second, we are faced with God's perspective on eternal values and how we can please Him and thus share in what He has provided. Third, in discovery Bible study we are involved actively in searching God's Word to master its contents and to harmonize our daily lives with its teachings. Fourth, this type of Bible study leads the learner to relate his deepest personal needs to God, to explore life's most vital issues in the light of God's revelation, and to live a life patterned after God's design and revealed will. Such a study begins at a very elementary level as one learns the basic doctrines and applies them to his life. With the passage of time, this study becomes even more challenging as new perspectives open up to us. The Holy Spirit takes us progressively onward from one level of faith to another as our Christian experience matures.

You may wonder if you have developed to the level of spiritual maturity where you can develop insights into God's truth which is revealed in the Bible. Before receiving new life in Christ, you may have been taught that only ministers, priests, or religious leaders who have received specialized training or have been given extraordinary spiritual authority can understand the Bible. But remember the divine resources God has made available to help us understand His Word. John 14:26 and 16:13 remind us that the Holy Spirit will help enable all Christians, including you, to understand God's truth. You must remember that the same divine Author who guided the revelation of truth initially is your Teacher and Guide in discovery Bible study (2 Peter 1:19-21). You can, and indeed must, study God's Word to hear what He is saying if you are to develop spiritually. And you must apply His truth to your own life if you expect to become a mature Christian. No one can do this for you. To help others grow toward spiritual maturity, then, you need to learn how to discover biblical truth for yourself and how to lead others to discover God's truth for application to their lives.

4 Circle the letter preceding each TRUE statement.

a Discovery involves inventing truth which did not exist previously.

b Discovery Bible study is a method of study which involves the learner actively in searching the Scriptures to learn what God is revealing so that he may respond obediently to Him.

c Discovery involves uncovering truth not previously known to the learner.

d Discovery Bible study is limited to knowing God's revealed truth.

e Only those called to be teachers should study the Bible.

f Discovery Bible study involves learning biblical content and harmonizing one's life with those teachings.

g The Holy Spirit will enable all Christians to understand God's truth.

Approaches to Discovery Bible Study

Objective 3. *Label diagrams correctly which show two approaches to discovery Bible study.*

In the previous section we saw that discovery Bible study involves four steps which may be summarized as follows:

1. Defining life needs
2. Discovering biblical truth
3. Deciding how to apply biblical truth to life needs
4. Doing (that is, implementing) God's Word in real life

The order of working through these steps determines which approach is used. For the purposes of our study, two approaches are indicated: the *systematic approach* and the *life-needs approach*. The *systematic approach* may be diagrammed as follows:

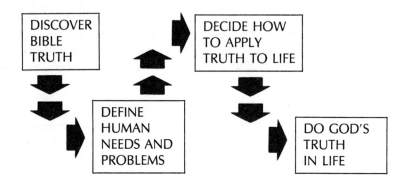

This approach is called systematic because it employs a systematic approach to the study of the Bible. You select a book or passage of Scripture and study it to learn what truth God has revealed in the passage. Then you ask yourself this question: How does this truth apply to my life needs? Finally, you implement your discoveries.

The *life needs approach* differs slightly and may be diagrammed as follows:

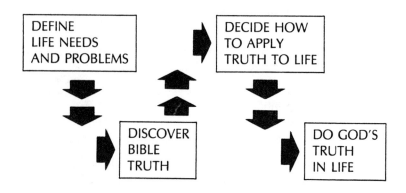

When following this approach you begin by probing life-related problems, by identifying your needs and interests. The next step is to look for Bible teachings which apply to the needs or become a basis for solving the problems. Then you link what you discover in your Bible study to your life needs. This forms a basis for solving your life problem. In the final step you implement your conclusions.

The basic difference between the two approaches is whether you begin with your needs and move to God's perspective or if you begin with a systematic approach to Scripture and move to life needs. Both approaches are valid and may be useful. The systematic approach may tend to result in a more in-depth knowledge of the passage being studied, but it may not contain the full teaching of Scripture on a given issue. The life-needs approach may lead you to consult a broader range of biblical teaching on a matter of concern, but it may not lead you to study areas of divine truth where you may not feel particular problems or needs. For this reason, many Bible scholars favor the systematic approach.

5 Label correctly the following diagrams to show the correct order of procedure for each approach to discovery Bible study, based upon our discussion in the preceding section.

a The Systematic Approach

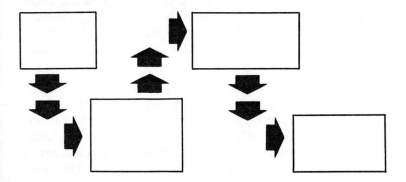

201

b The Life-Needs Approach

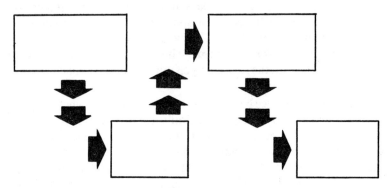

INDUCTIVE BIBLE STUDY

Tasks of Inductive Bible Study

Objective 4. *Choose statements which describe correctly the tasks of inductive Bible study.*

We have seen that in two approaches to discovery Bible study one must seek to discover biblical truth for himself and then endeavor to lead others to discover biblical truth for themselves. In our efforts to help others discover biblical truth we use an approach that is referred to as *inductive Bible study*.

Inductive Bible study is a method of studying Scripture by observing carefully what the text says, understanding what was meant by what was said, and applying that truth to our lives and times today. It involves direct *observation* of the biblical text, *interpretation* of what is stated, and *application* of the truth revealed to our lives.

Inductive Bible study involves us in two basic tasks: 1) discovering the message God intended for the original readers, and 2) determining how to apply that message properly to our lives today. In the first of these tasks, you and I are seeking to hear what God was saying to those who first received the message under consideration. The Bible was written centuries ago to specific people who lived in a particular part of the world and who understood certain conditions. To hear what they heard, you and I must seek to understand them, their times, how they lived, and what their conditions were. Their historical, geographical, cultural, and social settings are important keys that help us understand what they knew and what they heard as they read God's Word. Many times the messages of Scripture cannot be understood properly nor applied to our lives appropriately apart from a knowledge of these factors.

For example, without a knowledge of the context, one might just lift a biblical command out of its setting and do something never intended by our Lord. A case in point may be seen on the occasion when Jesus said to a man who was expert in the Law, "Go and do likewise" (Luke 10:37). Without a knowledge of Luke 10:25-37, one would not know that the man had asked just what he must do to inherit eternal life. Nor would he know that this question prompted Jesus to relate the Parable of the Good Samaritan. Thus, if by chance a person who wanted some justification for swearing were to read in turn Mark 14:71 and Luke 10:37 (concerning the command to go and do likewise), he might feel, wrongly that he had a full biblical warrant to swear. Obviously, this is not the intent of Jesus' statement in Luke 10:37, but some people do try to twist the Scriptures wherever possible to serve their own interests. We must avoid this practice as we correctly handle the word of truth (2 Timothy 2:15).

The second task involves us in applying the truth of Scripture to our lives within our own circumstances, cultures, and particular situations. We must recognize that we are not the ones to whom God's truth was originally revealed. It was not first of all addressed to us. The meaning of Scripture to us must grow out of what it meant originally. The Bible cannot mean to us what it never meant when it was given originally. Attempting to give new, deeper, or fuller meaning to Scripture other than what God originally intended is dangerous and has often led to heresy.

6 Circle the letter preceding each TRUE statement.

a The Bible was addressed primarily to you and me.

b Inductive Bible study involves discovering the original message of Scripture and then applying it appropriately to our lives.

c When we have an understanding of the times and settings of the people who first received the Word of God, we are better prepared to understand the message that was conveyed to them.

d The Bible's message should not be given meanings today which were not originally intended by God.

e Inductive Bible study involves direct observation of the original biblical text, interpretation of what is stated, and application to our lives.

Steps to Inductive Bible Study.

Objective 5. *Choose statements which correctly identify the three steps to inductive Bible study.*

The inductive method of Bible study takes us inside a passage of Scripture to discover its message and meaning. There are three basic steps to this method: 1) observation, 2) interpretation, and 3) application.

Observation calls for reading and rereading the passage several times. It requires looking, seeing, and noticing what is actually stated. Observation involves concentration on the words, their logical arrangement, and their grammatical usage. The following questions may help you discover truth in a passage: Who is the writer? To whom is the message addressed? What do we know about these people? When was the message written? What were the particular conditions or circumstances which occasioned the message? What is the central message of the book or passage? What is the writer saying generally? What is he saying specifically? Read the passage and observe what it says.

Interpretation of the written message involves us in the process of determining what the writer meant by what he said or wrote. The writer had a thought, an idea, or a concept in his mind. Through the medium of writing, he sought to communicate that message to those who would read what he wrote. The words are the vehicles which carry the idea from the writer's mind to the reader's mind. It is that idea, the message, which the reader should seek to understand. Any written message must be interpreted correctly to be understood. Interpretation is the process of determining accurately what a writer means by what he writes.

These two steps, observation and interpretation, lead us to accomplish the first task: discovering the message which was intended for the original readers. But the process does not end here. God speaks in the Scriptures not only to the original readers to whom the message was primarily addressed but also to us. Second Timothy 3:16-17 lets us know that there is an expanded use for all Scriptures: that the man of God (of all times) may grow and mature spiritually. Therefore, the goal of all Bible study is to hear the general principles which God has revealed to us and apply them in our particular set of life circumstances.

We discover what God is saying to us in His Word through the application of the truth to our lives and our needs. In applying the Scriptures we should look for direct commands which state general, spiritual principles that are to be obeyed by all Christians. We should also look for promises made by God and the conditions which must be met to receive those promises. And we should search for examples, either positive or negative, which may act as a guide for us. Sometimes God's requirements are explicitly stated, while at other times they take the form of principles which must be related to our circumstances. Some Bible passages identify attitudes and behaviors which are sinful. We should ask ourselves how these passages apply to our lives. If they reveal unworthy faults which are in evidence in our lives, then we must move swiftly to get rid of them. And we should seek to discover if there are things which we should be doing but are neglecting. Applying biblical truth to our lives involves relating it to our present life situations.

7-11 Circle the letter in front of the correct answer for each of the following questions, based on our discussion in this section.

7 How many steps are there to inductive Bible study?
a) Two
b) Three
c) Four
d) Five

8 Which one of the following is NOT involved in observation?
a) Reading
b) Looking
c) Discussing
d) Noticing

9 The purpose of observation of a biblical text is to
a) discover what the writer says.
b) decide if it contains a message.
c) find ways to apply truth to our lives.
d) find errors in the writer's work.

10 The purpose of interpretation is to
a) determine how to apply the message.
b) discover what words the writer used.
c) decide what to do about the message.
d) determine what the writer meant by what he wrote.

11 The purpose of application is to
a) discover what God is saying to us in the Scriptures.
b) determine what a biblical text means.
c) discover what a biblical text says.
d) decide why the writer wrote the message.

12 OPTIONAL ASSIGNMENT. To give you some practice in conducting an inductive Bible study, we have provided this optional assignment. Read the book of Jonah at least three times. Write answers to the questions listed above in the discussion about observation. Then find two or three statements in the book which describe some aspect of the nature and character of God and write them in your notebook. What do these truths say to you? How do they relate to your particular life situation? Write these applications in your notebook, also.

Inductive Bible study may be conducted by an individual or a group. As you prepare Bible studies to teach others you will employ the inductive Bible study approach. And as you teach, you will lead learners through the steps of inductive Bible study.

PLANNING LEARNING ENCOUNTERS

Objective 6. *Choose statements which tell correctly how to plan learning encounters.*

To help others discover biblical truth through inductive Bible study you will need to plan effective learning encounters. Planning learning encounters which enable learners to interact with the material and to discover God's truth is not difficult once you understand how to do it. The following diagram shows three essential steps to follow in planning learning encounters:

DETERMINE LEARNING OBJECTIVES		DESIGN LEARNING ACTIVITIES		EVALUATE LEARNER PROGRESS

Learning objectives grow out of the interests and needs of learners and the content of the material being studied. Determining learning objectives is a matter of determining in advance the changes you want to see in learners. Based on the material being studied and the needs of learners, what changes would you like to see take place? The learning objectives should state what learners should be able to do after instruction that they could not do before. The changes should occur in each of the areas you studied in Lesson 4—knowledge, attitudes, and behavior.

We have stated objectives at the beginning of each lesson in this course. These can serve as examples to you of how to state learning objectives. Study them carefully.

Once you have determined what changes you want to occur in the learners, you are ready to design activities to enable those changes to take place. The task here is to move the learner from where he is to the place you want him to be—where the objectives state he should be. Here you are choosing appropriate teaching methods, planning learner assignments, and deciding how to use the available time to produce the desired changes. These activities should lead the student to interact with the material in a meaningful way. They should lead him to see the possible applications of the truth to his own life.

Since learning is the goal of the teaching-learning situation, the emphasis in designing learning activities should be on what the learners will do rather than on what the teacher will do. This is one of the major areas where we must keep in mind that the learner must encounter the material personally and interact with it for himself. Consequently, designing learning encounters involves planning ways to induce the learner to encounter and interact with the material.

The final step is to evaluate the learner's progress. This is done by comparing the learner's actual progress with the intended progress. The intended progress is stated in the learning objectives. Hence, the learning objectives become the criteria for evaluating learner progress. Did he make the desired changes? To what extent did he make those changes?

There are several ways to determine if the desired changes were actually made. One common way is to administer a test. Test questions may be either of the objective type, in which the answers are either correct or incorrect, or they may be of the subjective type, in which the learner states his responses in his own words. True-false, multiple choice, and matching type questions are of the objective type, while essay and short-answer questions are of the subjective type.

Another way for you to evaluate learner progress is through personal observation of learner behavior. This calls for you to see if the learner actually uses the material in real-life situations.

You can also determine the progress the learner is making through the learning encounters by means of an interview. As you talk with him, you may be able to see evidence of growth and change. While this may be a subjective thing, it, nevertheless, can be a valid means of determining learner progress.

13 Circle the letter in front of each TRUE statement.
a The primary concern of any learning encounter is what interests the student.
b Effective learning encounters take into consideration both the needs of the learner and the changes you desire to see take place in his life.
c Learning objectives help us plan activities that will enable learners to make the changes we want to see them make.
d Learning objectives give us a means of measuring whether or not the desired changes have occurred.
e By their very nature, learning encounters require little or no learner involvement beyond hearing and understanding the content being studied.

14 In designing learning activities, the emphasis should be on
a) what procedures the teacher will follow, what he will do.
b) how long the activities will take and whether they will fill the allotted class time.
c) what the learners will do, how they will interact with the material.

15 We may evaluate learners' progress by doing which of the following, based on the foregoing discussion?
a) Testing them to see whether they know verbatim all the content they were given
b) Testing them to see their actual progress as compared to the intended progress
c) Comparing their present progress with their condition at the beginning of the learning encounters
d) Comparing their condition with that of an ideal Christian model as defined in the writings of the apostle Paul

self-test

TRUE-FALSE. In front of each question write **T** if the statement is TRUE, **F** if it is FALSE.

.... **1** According to this lesson, the four activities which satisfactorily define the *teaching task* are: story telling, stating facts, describing events, and explaining information.

.... **2** Researchers no longer refer to the *teaching task* because discovery learning means that students are fully self-taught.

.... **3** The teaching task involves creating a learning environment, motivating students to learn, and guiding the students' discovery of knowledge.

.... **4** Structuring learning opportunities, planning activities which require the student to interact with the materials, and designing learning experiences which lead to change are functions of the teaching task.

.... **5** Behavior changes indicate that learning has occurred.

.... **6** Discovery Bible study implies that the learner discovers truth which has never existed previously.

.... **7** In discovery Bible study the learner searches the Scriptures to learn what God is revealing so that he may respond obediently.

.... **8** The Holy Spirit enables a learner to understand God's truth in the discovery study method.

.... **9** Learning occurs in the discovery study method only if the four steps of learning are followed in order.

....**10** The *systematic approach* to Bible study requires learning what is revealed accurately in a passage of Scripture, knowing its application in life, and implementing the discovery.

....**11** The *life needs approach* involves identifying needs and interests, discovering Bible teachings which apply to and solve the problems, and applying the truth.

....**12** Inductive Bible study involves two basic tasks: 1) discovering what God intended for us in the biblical revelation, and 2) determining whether it applies to us specifically.

....**13** According to the lesson, there are three basic steps to inductive Bible study: 1) observation, 2) interpretation, and 3) application.

....**14** Once you have determined the interests and needs of learners, you can plan effective learning encounters by determining learning objectives, designing appropriate learning activities, and then evaluating learners' progress.

....**15** In a meaningful learning encounter, the emphasis should be on what procedures the teacher will follow, what he will do.

This is the final lesson in Unit 2. After you have taken the self-test, review Lessons 4 through 7 and answer the questions in unit student report 2. Follow the directions given in the unit student report booklet.

---

answers to study questions

8 c) Discussing.

1 b) Guiding.
   c) Structuring.
   e) Motivating.
   f) Planning.
   g) Creating.
   i) Facilitating.

9 a) discover what the writer says.

2 a guide
  b discover, apply

10 d) determine what the writer meant by what he wrote.

3 Your answer may be different from mine, but it should include similar ideas. Change indicates that the learner has heard and understood the message and that he is applying what he learned. Change demonstrates that learning has occurred.

11 a) discover what God is saying to us in the Scriptures.

4 a False.
  b True.
  c True.
  d False.
  e False.
  f True.
  g True.

12 Your answers.

5 a Discover Bible truth.
    Define human needs and problems.
    Decide how to apply truth to life.
    Do God's truth in life.
  b Define life needs and problems.
    Discover Bible truth.
    Decide how to apply truth to life.
    Do God's truth in life.

13 a False.
  b True.
  c True.
  d True.
  e False.

 6 a False.
  b True.
  c True.
  d True.
  e ~~False.~~ TRUE

14 c) What the learners will do, how they will interact with the material.

 7 b) Three.

15 b) Testing them to see their actual progress.
  c) Comparing their present progress.

Unit 3

GROWING WITH OTHERS

LESSON 8

Growing in Families

One hot afternoon Juan was busily making repairs on the car. Close by was Manuel, watching his father work. The tool Juan was using slipped, causing him to hurt his hand and to cry out in pain. In play the next day, Manuel pretended to repair his bicycle with the same tool he had seen his father using. Maria was watching him play when the tool slipped in his hand also. She heard Manuel cry the very same words his father used the day before.

That evening Maria told Juan what she had seen happening with Manuel. They discussed the importance of their personal influence in the life of their son. Since both parents wanted Manuel to grow up to become a well-adjusted, responsible adult, they prayed together that God would help them always to set the right example before their son.

Perhaps you have had a similar experience in your home. Can you recall imitating something you saw one of your parents do? Or maybe you have seen one of your own children copy your behavior. This lesson is about the nurturing which takes place in the home. The purpose of nurturing is to help individuals develop into wholeness and maturity in the likeness of Christ. The family unit is one of the most important places where nurturing takes place. God's Word has much to say about this important subject which can give direction to your life and ministry. May its importance be impressed upon you as you in turn seek to build the body of Christ through the various nurturing ministries.

lesson outline

The Biblical View of Marriage
The Nature of Families

lesson objectives

When you finish this lesson you should be able to:

■ Discuss the biblical view of marriage.

■ Describe how to help marriages grow.

■ Describe two major tasks of Christian parents.

■ Describe two kinds of experiences which contribute to family-life nurture.

learning activities

1. Study the lesson according to the procedure recommended in Lesson 1.

2. After you have completed the lesson development section, take the self-test and check your answers.

key words

admonition   monogamous
complement   polygamous
endearing   social identity
familiarity   tyrant
gratifying

lesson development

THE BIBLICAL VIEW OF MARRIAGE

God's Design

Objective 1. *Identify God's purpose in creating man, how man differs from other creatures, why woman was created, the helping concept of marriage, and the purpose of the family.*

The first two chapters of Genesis tell of the marvelous creative acts of God. This account includes the creation of the heavens and the earth. It reveals God's placement of the sun, moon, and stars in the heavens and their purpose. We learn that He filled the earth with many beautiful and different kinds of plants, each capable of reproducing itself. Moreover, we see that He filled the land, sea, and sky with a fascinating variety of creatures, bringing His creative acts almost to completion. Then, when He reviewed all that He had done, God said that it was very good.

God's final, crowning act of creation was the making of man. Man was to be made in the image of his Creator. To this point, God had not made any creature or plant like Him. Now, however, from the dust of the earth God shaped a body and breathed life into it. This creature, patterned after the Creator, was man. He was different

220

from all other creatures, because he was a moral being: he had the ability to know and choose between good and evil. In this way he was like his Maker. He also had the ability to communicate with God.

Man was different from other creatures not only because he was a moral being, but because he was *alone.* All other creatures were created as pairs, male and female, but man labored in the Garden of Eden by himself. Then God said, "It is not good for the man to be alone. I will make a helper suitable for him" (Genesis 2:18). Thus, God took a part of the man's side and made a woman to be his companion. She was to be his helper and share the responsibility of caring for the Garden. She was to complement her husband's efforts, provide companionship for him, and with him populate the earth.

God created man in a very special way for a very special purpose: He could respond to God's love and glorify Him. In addition, we learn that God made the human pair with the capacity for a special relationship. The husband-wife relationship was designed to be the basic relationship in a family and one which provides social identity. Since God created the man and the woman for each other, we see that He is the one who designed the family.

The Genesis account emphasizes that the husband-wife relationship is a helping one. God intended for husbands and wives to live together in such a way that the needs of each would be met. They have the capacity to relate to and share the emotional, intellectual and spiritual experiences of life. In addition, marriage provides for the most intimate physical relationship possible between marriage partners. God blessed this union and made it possible for the man and the woman to reproduce and populate the earth.

We see, then, that in addition to caring for creation and each other's needs, God's purpose for Adam and Eve was to have children. The ability to bear and rear children is a natural function of human life. While Adam and Eve were to share the most intimate relationship with each other, they were also to develop a loving relationship with their children. As parents, they were to provide a family setting in which they could nurture their children in the fear and admonition of God. Their lives and their teaching were to be an expression of their love for and trust in God. In this way their children would have an appropriate model. The children could thus grow into mature adulthood and eventually raise their own families by the same principles that had guided their parents.

The Bible clearly shows that from the beginning of history nurturing is an important part of the husband-wife and the parent-child relationship. It also reveals that nurturing in the family is God's plan. Through precept and example, a pattern for family life emerges from the Scriptures. It is summed up well in Proverbs 22:6, "Train up a child in the way he should go, and when he is old he will not turn from it." The suggestion is that God designed families to provide helpful nurturing relationships so that individuals can develop to wholeness and find fulfillment.

1-5 Based on the foregoing text, circle the letter preceding the correct answer for each one of the following questions.

1 God's purpose in creating man was to (select the best answer)
a) provide a caretaker for the created order.
b) make one who could respond to His directives and glorify Him.
c) provide for the population of the earth.

2 Man differs from all other created beings in what way(s)?
a) Man alone of all creatures has the ability to think.
b) Man was made in the image of God.
c) Man differs from other creatures only in the sense that he is more complex.

3 God created woman for all of the following reasons but one. Circle the letter in front of the one which is NOT stated in the foregoing discussion.
a) Woman was created to be man's helper.
b) The woman God created was to complement man's abilities and to help fulfill God's plan for creation.
c) Woman was created to occupy both a subordinate and an inferior role in the created order.
d) Through nurture and example woman was to help rear God-fearing children and thus perpetuate the race.

4 The helping concept of the marriage is that
a) woman is fulfilled in her subordinate relationship to man.
b) as the husband and wife meet each other's needs, God's purpose is fulfilled in that relationship.
c) as each member of the marital unit insists on the help of the other member, the needs of each will be met.

5 God designed the family to (circle the letter preceding the most complete answer)
a) provide nurturing relationships as man populated and cared for the earth.
b) populate the earth, enjoy its fruits, and care for it.
c) provide social order and government for the people He had created.

The Nature of Marriage

Objective 2. *Match words such as* nurturing, caring, loving, intimate, and oneness *to their meanings in the context of this lesson.*

The marriage relationship is so special that it is recognized in all societies by certain means. Often the marriage of a couple is formalized by either a civil or religious ceremony or by a customary ritual. Whether rites are elaborate or simple, some procedure is usually followed which formally recognizes a man and a woman as a basic family unit: husband and wife.

The marriage of a man and a woman is based upon certain expectations and commitments between them. If you will review carefully Genesis 1:26-28 and 2:20-25, you will find several factors which characterize the marriage relationship.

1. Marriage was ordained by God as a relationship only between a man and a woman. God designed them for each other in a special way. This is the natural sexual order God intended.

2. Marriage is an intimate relationship which is viewed as a "oneness" between the man and woman. This is revealed in the way

God made woman from a part of man's side. This is an excellent illustration of the unity which should be found in marriage. Adam saw Eve as a vital part of his own body. When God made Eve's body, He designed it differently from the body He had shaped for Adam. The very difference in their bodies prepared them for physical intimacy with each other. In every way God prepared each of them for intimacy with the other.

3. Marriage is a monogamous relationship. While many cultures recognize and permit polygamous marriages, the Bible does not show this to be true with Adam and Eve. The major emphasis which is seen in the Bible is that God intended marriage to be between one man and one woman.

4. Marriage is to be a permanent relationship. Husband and wife are to be united until one of them dies. In marriage they are united as one flesh in a covenant before God, and that commitment is binding between them so long as they both live.

5. Marriage marks the beginning of a new family unit. When a man and woman are united as husband and wife, this establishes a new family with an identity different from the family in which either was born and raised. Moreover, social recognition is given to this new unit and the laws of marriage and property now apply. In some cultures the new husband and wife no longer live with their parents. Instead they establish a new home and begin having their own children.

6. Marriage is a comfortable trusting relationship. There should be no shame between the husband and wife. The Bible refers to this in Genesis 2:25. Even though they were naked, Adam and Eve felt no shame. They were aware of their differences, but they were fully satisfied in the innocence and purity of their commitment to each other.

From the Genesis record it is clear that God designed a loving, intimate, and fulfilling relationship which He wanted a husband and wife to share with each other. This relationship was to express love and provide a basis for nurturing and caring for each other. Such an environment would be the natural setting in which children could be reared to appreciate the blessings of God on their home and in each aspect of their lives.

6 Match each word (right) to its appropriate definition or meaning (left) as used in the context of this lesson.

....a Refers to the way in which one spouse watches out for the needs of the other. Also speaks of one's concern.

....b Refers to the closeness and intimacy brought about by the marriage union.

....c Refers to the consideration one has for his spouse. Also refers to the training, discipline, and support of one's children.

....d Refers to close association, familiarity, or contact; of a very personal or private nature

....e Refers to the expressions of affection, tenderness, and devotion one has for another.

1) Nurturing
2) Caring
3) Loving
4) Intimate
5) Oneness

Nurturing in Marriage

Objective 3. *Identify the behaviors of husbands and wives which nurture the marriage.*

The marriage relationship originally established by God and reaffirmed to Adam and Eve after their sin continues today. The apostle Paul teaches that the husband is the head, or leader, of the wife and the home (1 Corinthians 11:3). He also affirms that husbands and fathers are basically responsible to provide for the needs of their families. If a man won't support his family, then he is to be considered worse than someone who does not even believe

225

in God (1 Timothy 5:8). We must not forget that Paul is speaking to Christian husbands and wives in these Scriptures.

The story of Adam and Eve which we have considered in Genesis 1 and 2 continues in chapters 3 and 4. As you read these chapters, you will see that Adam and Eve made a serious mistake which was to affect every aspect of their lives. No longer could they remain in the Garden of Eden where there was an abundance of food and lovely flowers. Because of their sin in disobeying God's commands, they were forced to leave the Garden and live and work in a place filled with thorns. Now they had to toil and labor just to have food and a place to live. Their position in relation to the created order had changed. Thus, instead of being responsible for it they became slaves to it. Because of this sin, their relationship changed with each other, also. Eve had been created to be her husband's helper, but now God placed Adam as the leader of the home. In addition, Eve now had to endure much suffering when she gave birth to her children. Because of Adam's sin the ground was cursed. The abundance he had known in the Garden was gone. Henceforth he would have to work very hard to support his wife and family. Sin also became the basis of the problems that arose in their marriage relationship.

The marriage relationship is regarded by God as a sacred one. Jesus refers to the husband-wife relationship as one in which God has joined two people together (Mark 10:9). Since God created all things to be good, we can conclude that marriage was intended to be a good association. Not only did God ordain marriage, but He also gave instructions in His Word to husbands and wives about how they could live together and make their home happier.

It is especially important that married people learn the basic teachings of God's Word about marriage if they are to have a loving, nurturing relationship. Specific instructions are given to the husband and wife, teaching them how to live before each other honorably and effectively as Christian believers. Let us first consider the teachings given to the husbands.

Instructions to Husbands

In speaking to the family relationship, the apostle Paul admonished each husband to love his wife in a way which is patterned after the way Christ loves His church. When you genuinely love someone, you sincerely care about that person and you want only the best for her. Your love will cause you to do everything in your power to take care of her and to think of her welfare before you think of your own. Christ demonstrated His love for the church by dying to redeem the ones He loved and to make them presentable to Him. Husbands should have this caring attitude also.

A man who loves his wife and family works to support them. He uses his skills and abilities to provide food, shelter, and clothing for them. A loving husband does not forget nor neglect his responsibilities to his family.

A loving husband cares about his wife's feelings. A husband who loves his wife does not talk or think badly about her. Instead, he says and does things which express his love for her. He does not abuse her for her mistakes and faults, but in patience and love he seeks to help her find solutions for these problems. His understanding and patience creates a favorable environment in which improvement is likely to occur.

A husband who truly loves his wife cares enough about her to understand her emotional needs. He takes the time to talk about the problems that concern her. He expresses his love for her and does all he can to make her feel secure in her relationship with him. He gives her the emotional support necessary to help her be a better wife and mother.

One who loves his wife and appreciates her role in the family unit seeks to nurture her spiritually. The wife should see in her husband a person who loves God and provides an example for the family to follow in serving and worshiping God. He takes the lead in family devotions, helps in the neighborhood as a Christian neighbor, serves in the church as a vital part of the body, and applies the Word continually to life situations. Above all, he upholds his wife and family in prayer, thanking God for them and for the privilege of being a steward of the things of God. God is pleased when a man leads his family in this manner.

A wife draws security from the marital relationship when she realizes that she is a vital part of her husband's life and that he loves her. She draws additional assurance when he expresses confidence in her opinion when decisions need to be made which affect her and the family. The husband nurtures his wife by esteeming her as the most important person in his life. The knowledge that she is needed and wanted is a vital part of the marriage-family relationship.

Another important way a husband provides nurturing support and love for his wife is by helping her in her role as a parent. The husband and father should teach his children that they are to love, respect, and obey their mother. A loving husband never permits his wife to suffer reproach or abuse from the children. The wife must know that she has the backing of her husband in the family as she establishes and enforces rules for the home as she disciplines the children.

Paul emphasizes the duty of the husband to care for the sexual needs of his wife. In 1 Corinthians 7:3-5 he instructs husbands not to withhold themselves sexually from their wives except by mutual consent for a temporary period of time. The Scriptures teach that sexual intimacy is a part of the marital contract between a husband and wife, and it should not be used in a negative, selfish way against a spouse. To refuse to be sexually intimate with one's wife opens the doors for Satan to tempt both the husband and wife to sin in this area of their lives.

Instructions for Wives

The wife is also given instructions about her relationship with the husband. Paul teaches that the wife should submit herself to her own husband (Ephesians 5:22). In this context, the implication is that the husband is to exercise the leadership role in the family. The wife demonstrates submission by recognizing and accepting her husband's leadership role, acknowledging through this the divine order for the family and therefore, the authority of God in her life. Submission is not meant to imply that the woman is inferior to her husband, nor is it intended to be a license for the husband to behave as a tyrant toward his wife. Submission is the recognition of the roles God has given for family life. The husband has been taught to give his love to his wife, but the wife has to be willing to receive it if his love is to be effective in her life.

The wife has a nurturing role in the marriage in the way she relates to her husband. Her husband needs to know that she appreciates his efforts to provide for her. She should express her appreciation for his efforts, provision, and concern in ways that let him know she is mindful of all his leadership entails. She can also be supportive by using wisely the family resources which she handles. Moreover, her ability to stand by her husband faithfully when he faces problems and set-backs will lend the kind of loving encouragement that is necessary in hard times.

A loving wife tries to make the home a pleasant and restful place for her husband. A clean home, prompt meals, and a pleasant, loving attitude toward the responsibilities of the home show the husband that his wife cares deeply about him. A wife who approaches her responsibilities in this way will undoubtedly find that her husband will respond in a loving and caring manner toward her too.

The committed Christian wife will nurture her husband as he leads the home and family in the worship and service of God. She will indicate her support of his leadership through the high value she places on spiritual things in the home as well as in the church. Such a wife will keep her relationship right with God so that it will make her relationship with her husband better. This harmony in the home will be an appropriate testimony to their family of the practicality and reality of true Christian living and it will speak to neighbors as well. It will make their service to God in their local church more effective, for their lives will reflect the love, peace, and joy of God which flows out of their daily lives.

A husband has emotional and physical needs that a Christian wife will be concerned about. She will want to do all she can to be supportive of her husband, showing him that she cares about his needs and that he can depend on her. She will lovingly provide the intimacy necessary to enrich her relationship with her husband. As Paul told the husband to be mindful of his wife's sexual needs, he also gave the same instruction to the wife regarding the husband's sexual needs (1 Corinthians 7:3-5). Through sexual intimacy, the wife can express her full acceptance of her husband and give to him her deepest affections. In turn she will probably find that as she meets her husband's needs, he will respond positively to meet hers.

From our examination of the Ephesians passage, we see that God wants Christian marriage and home life to be happy and fulfilling. The responsibility for these rests equally on each spouse. Each one is to nurture the relationship carefully and willfully so that it will lead to a happy home and an abundant life together.

7 Based upon our discussion in this section, circle the letter preceding each TRUE statement in the following exercise.

a Husbands nurture their families as they support them, providing the necessities of life.

b When a husband provides the physical needs of his family members, he has done all that is required to nurture them toward wholeness.

c Nurturing includes caring for the emotional, spiritual, intellectual, and social needs of one's family.

d Husbands and wives need not express their appreciation for their spouses; nurturing is accomplished fully as they perform their duties without showing affection or expressing love openly.

e Nurturing is demonstrated as a husband gives his support to the role of the wife in her duties as a parent.

f The marriage relationship is nurtured as the wife accepts the leadership role of her husband, and this is strengthened as she expresses her appreciation for his efforts.

g Whether the wife does her work well, makes the home cheerful and clean, and administers the affairs of the home well or not is unimportant as long as she accepts her husband's leadership role.

h Nurturing occurs as each marital partner provides for the intimacy necessary to enrich the marriage relationship.

THE NATURE OF FAMILIES

Objective 4. *Choose a definition of the term family which shows correctly its nature and function.*

When the word family is mentioned, many people may think of the home in which they were born and reared. If you are an adult not living with your parents, perhaps you can recall some special event or custom which was practiced by your parents when you were a child. If so, this event probably still brings fond memories to your mind. The term family has a special, endearing meaning for many people. It is the social unit in which our life began and it continues to influence us in important ways.

231

In Genesis 1:28 you will note that God wanted Adam and Eve to have children. Children are viewed in Scripture as a part of God's heritage and blessing in life. They are His reward (Psalm 127:3). In Proverbs 17:6 we are told that grandchildren are a blessing and that the glory of the child is in his "fathers" (or ancestry). God's design for the family is this: a husband and wife are to become a father and mother. This is as He ordained it and it is good and right.

Children normally live with their mother and father and brothers and sisters until they become adults. There may be an age in your culture when children begin to leave their parents' home and establish homes of their own. As adults, they are expected to earn their own living and provide for their own needs. This is the natural progression in life.

However, before children reach the age when they would normally leave their parents, they live in a family. Some cultures may have different family unit arrangements. Children may be cared for by persons other than the parents. These may be uncles and aunts or grandparents. The child soon learns who is responsible for his needs, and he depends on them for food, shelter, protection, and security. Parents have certain duties and obligations for a child during his developing years. However, when the child becomes an adult, he assumes these responsibilities for himself. And parents teach their children during their childhood and adolescence how to take care of themselves, act responsibly, and prepare for their role as adults.

Since most of the years of a person's life are lived as an adult, we must give special attention and training during the pre-adult years. The basic lessons in life are usually learned in the home. Our first teachers are usually our parents. A strong bond of love and intimacy should be developed between the parents and the child. This bond of love and caring should continue all through a person's life. The parent-child relationship is very special and provides meaning and guidance for a lifetime.

We see the nature of the family in every culture. In each a cycle of life can be observed. Children are born as tiny, helpless infants to their parents. As they begin to grow and mature, they are taught the lessons of life which are important for the adult years. There is usually an age when the maturing son or daughter is regarded as adult. Each is now required to behave responsibly as an adult member of the society. The marriage of these young adults normally produces children, and the cycle begins again.

8 Based on our discussion of the family, circle the letter preceding the most correct definition of the term family.
a) The term *family* refers to any group of persons which is joined together by common interests, backgrounds, education, and language.
b) The term *family* refers to a class of people which acts together to promote the common good.
c) The term *family* refers to the most basic human social unit which can both reproduce life and prepare and influence that person for productive and meaningful life.

Nurturing in Families

Objective 5. *Identify examples of proper environment, example, explanation, teaching-learning situations, and the rationale for discipline in family nurturing.*

Perhaps you can recall the previous discussion in this lesson about the effect of sin on marriage. The results of that sin by Adam and Eve brought serious problems into their family for them as parents and for their children. Many ideas and teachings exist about the proper way parents should rear their children. However, for Christian parents, the best teachings are to be found in the Bible. These are the instructions given by the One who designed the family. As such, these lessons should naturally provide the best information.

In Ephesians 6:4, fathers are instructed to rear their children in the "nurture and admonition of the Lord." *Nurture* is a term that has several related meanings. It means to educate with good instruction and training. It also includes disciplinary correction as a means to assist the learning process.

Parents are further instructed to teach their children in the "admonition of the Lord." To admonish means to call children's attention to something on purpose. The parent may have to use a rebuke or warning in order to help the child learn. To admonish also implies that children are to be trained and taught in every part of their being. They learn physical discipline as they develop their motor skills in work and play. They are taught to develop their intellectual abilities. Children are given the proper instruction about how to express themselves emotionally. And certainly they are given thorough teaching which will cause them to mature spiritually.

Growth to maturity is a learning process. Children receive new understanding from several sources. They can be nurtured by the environment, by example, and by explanation. All of these areas of learning are important and parents can use them effectively to train the child properly.

Children learn many lessons just from the environment in which they live and develop toward maturity. Parents can increase their effectiveness in nurturing their children by providing the kind of setting in the home that will contribute to the learning process. Christian parents can do much to develop a Christian atmosphere. Music, reading materials, toys and games, art, and wholesome forms of entertainment are just a few things which influence children and have a teaching impact on them. Have you noticed how a child begins to imitate the sounds which are around him? Perhaps he hears a song on the television or radio, and later the parents hear him trying to sing the same song. The Christian influence can readily be a part of the child's life if parents will fill the environment with those things which impart or influence the Christian message. These things usually have a positive impact on the child.

Parents have the wonderful opportunity to nurture their children by the example of their own lives. Children are very impressionable. What they see their parents doing is going to be viewed as what is right. Very quickly they will begin to imitate their parents' behavior and actions. Christian parents who lovingly nurture their children will strive to teach biblical truth by their personal example. The example of the parents has a long-term impact on their children. Quite often children continue to be influenced by parental examples even after they become adults.

Christian parents have the obligation and opportunity to nurture their children by explaining what they should learn. Children are blessed and greatly benefited by sitting with parents and having the Bible stories read and explained to them. The lessons of Scripture are lessons of life for children. They learn quickly to judge their own behavior by the examples from the Scripture. Their minds begin to develop an understanding of the basic life-giving truth of God's Word. This knowledge becomes the basis for understanding the moral laws of God. This growing knowledge of God's Word which begins in childhood can, and usually does, have an effect which reaches into the adult years.

The proper nurturing of children requires that parents discipline and correct their behavior in a loving and caring manner. As the children grow, the parents will notice that they will increasingly seek to have their own way. Quite often, children do misbehave. God has commanded that children obey their parents and honor them (Ephesians 6:1). It is the parents' responsibility to teach the children what is right and wrong and then to require that the children obey their teachings. It is not good for children to disobey their parents and not receive proper corrective discipline. Parents have an obligation before God to nurture their children with the type of discipline that both teaches and corrects them. The result of this kind of discipline is that children develop the strength to exercise self-discipline when they become adults.

The purpose of nurturing in the family is to develop those qualities of life in children which will bring them to maturity and wholeness. Most important is the development of the child's knowledge and understanding about God and His Word. This provides a solid basis for moral reasoning and judgment. Children must also learn how to be good, responsible members of their society and community. They should be nurtured in such a way that they are prepared to teach and train their own children someday.

While the most basic nurturing should occur in the family setting, additional nurturing should take place in the church setting, where the family worships together with other families. Children need to see the value of each family as it is faithful in its witness and service in its community. They should be led to see the church as a place of spiritual learning, corporate worship, fellowship, and service. The example parents set in terms of their church attendance and their support of its ministries will undoubtedly form a life-long influence on their children.

9 Write 1) in front of each statement that is appropriate for family nurturing and 2) in front of those that are not, based on our discussion.

.... **a** In Christian homes proper nurture includes love, instructions, example, and appropriate warning, but discipline is not necessary.

.... **b** As long as there is adequate teaching, good parental example, and regular church attendance, the home environment is not especially important.

.... **c** Nurturing, in the final analysis, is preparation for life.

.... **d** Nurturing involves intellectual, physical, emotional, and spiritual development.

.... **e** Christian parents teach by example as much as by their instruction; therefore, they must be aware of their conduct at all times.

.... **f** The instructions and explanation of Scripture which parents give to their children helps children apply God's Word to their own conduct and to the issues of life.

.... **g** One of the great characteristics of a Christian parent's love is his ability to ignore his children's disobedience, to act as if he didn't see or hear the disobedient behavior.

.... **h** If the home is truly effective in its nurturing activities, church attendance is unnecessary or optional.

Conclusion

Nurturing in the family relationships has a very important emphasis in God's Word. God designed these relationships: the relationship of marriage and that of being parents and children. His Word gives us adequate and important teachings about the way to develop a happy and joyful home. Christian husbands and wives will discover that their marriages will be much more meaningful and gratifying as each seeks to please God first and then his or her spouse. Parents who value the Christian teachings and who instill God's truth in their children from a very early age will usually discover that their children grow to be more responsible and better adjusted in life as adults.

self-test

TRUE-FALSE. Place a **T** in the blank space in front of each **TRUE** statement and an **F** in front of each **FALSE** statement.

.... **1** The only way man was different from other creatures was that God created him alone, without a mate.

.... **2** Adam designed the plan for family life after God created Eve.

.... **3** The purpose of the family is to provide nurturing relationships as mankind populates and cares for the earth.

.... **4** There is a major emphasis in the Bible on marriage as a relationship between one man and one woman which is to last until one of them dies.

.... **5** The Christian husband is commanded to love his wife with the same unselfish love that Christ showed for the church.

.... **6** One way a wife nurtures her husband is by standing by him in times of discouragement and setback and by encouraging him with her spiritual values.

.... **7** To admonish means to scold a child when he has made a mistake.

.... **8** Parents can more effectively nurture children by developing a Christian atmosphere with the aid of music, reading materials, toys, games, art, and wholesome forms of entertainment.

.... **9** The Christian who will make the strongest impression upon children as the model they should follow will be the chief elder of the church.

....**10** The primary goal in disciplining children is to have a peaceful home.

answers to study questions

5 a) provide nurturing relationships.

1 b) make one who could respond.

6 a 2) Caring.
  b 5) Oneness.
  c 1) Nurturing.
  d 4) Intimate.
  e 3) Loving.

2 b) Man was made in the image of God.

7 a True.
  b False.
  c True.
  d False.
  e True.
  f True.
  g False.
  h True.

3 c) Woman was created to occupy both a subordinate and an inferior role in the created order.

8 c) The term *family* refers to the most basic human social unit.

4 b) As the husband and wife meet each other's needs.

9 a 2) Not appropriate.
  b 2) Not appropriate.
  c 1) Appropriate.
  d 1) Appropriate.
  e 1) Appropriate.
  f 1) Appropriate.
  g 2) Not appropriate.
  h 2) Not appropriate.

LESSON 9

Growing in Sharing Groups

Juan had always enjoyed discussing the weather and the progress of his crops with the other farmers in the area. Maria, likewise, found great pleasure in meeting with groups of ladies to share news about their children and exchange recipes and household hints. So neither was very surprised when Manuel responded to his grandfather's question by stating that the thing he enjoyed most about going to school was getting to play with the other children.

We humans are social beings and need each other. We support and help one another. We learn and grow in group settings.

Spiritual growth, also, is helped by association with other Christians. The local church meets the need for association in corporate worship, fellowship, instruction, and service. However, smaller sharing groups provide a more informal basis for associating and tend to involve believers more personally in the process of nurturing spiritual life. Both forms of association are needed, and the smaller group should always complement the ministry of the local church.

In this lesson you will study the significance of sharing groups, how they minister to people's needs, and how to organize and conduct sharing group meetings. As you relate to a sharing group, you will see that it provides opportunities for you to learn from others and to help them develop toward Christlikeness.

lesson outline

Sharing Christ's Life in Small Groups
Identifying Principles of Group Effectiveness
Leading Sharing Groups

lesson objectives

When you finish this lesson you should be able to:

- State the purpose of Christian sharing groups.

- Discuss four interpersonal needs of people which are met through participation in Christian sharing groups.

- Explain some principles of group effectiveness.

- Identify some of the practical aspects of organizing and leading Christian sharing groups.

241

learning activities

1. Study the lesson development according to the procedure recommended in Lesson 1.

2. Look up the meanings of any key words that are unfamiliar to you.

3. When you have completed the lesson development, take the self-test and check your answers.

key words

affirm	innovation	significant
amenable	nonverbal	others
charismatic	punctuation	visual gestures
dynamically	optimum	visual
group dynamics	seclusion	punctuation
inhibited		

lesson development

SHARING CHRIST'S LIFE IN SMALL GROUPS

The Purpose of Sharing Groups

Objective 1. *Choose statements which indicate appropriately the purpose of sharing groups.*

All Christians have something in common: they have received new spiritual life, the life of Jesus. As you have studied this course, you have been made aware of the need of every Christian to nurture his spiritual life. This lesson introduces another element which contributes to spiritual growth. Because we Christians share in common the life of Jesus, we are related to each other. All who share this life are parts of His body (1 Corinthians 12:12, 27). This means that all Christians are vitally and dynamically related to each other.

This relationship may be impersonal and unmeaningful, unless it is developed; it should grow and develop, for that is the nature of the body, as we have seen.

We are responsible not only for each other's personal growth and development but also for the growth of our corporate experience. The church becomes strong and productive through the growth and vitality of its individual parts. All of these individual parts are working together for the overall purpose of the body. The natural body functions in a healthy, productive way as each part performs its specific task. In a spiritual sense, the body of Christ functions effectively as each individual growing member contributes his share. One of the most effective ways for this development to occur is through sharing groups. We shall see what occurs when members of sharing groups bring their commitment, energy, and labor to the church. Sharing groups can promote local church functions: glorify God, extend His kingdom, and edify and mature members of His body. Christians, therefore, should meet together to share the life of Christ and the fellowship of His body.

One important and meaningful way to promote spiritual growth and development is through small sharing groups. Small sharing groups of from 10-12 people are devoted to fellowship, intercessory prayer for each other, the mutual ministry of God's Word, and the sharing of spiritual resources. They provide an important environment in which spiritual growth can occur. The relationships which develop in such groups are valuable resources for nurturing the life of Christ in each member which develops spiritual maturity. These group relationships make it possible for each member to draw strength and support from all other members and to contribute to the spiritual development of others. Members of small sharing groups can affirm each other so that each may grow spiritually, and in the process the corporate experience of the group is enriched also.

Such rich fellowship, interpersonal relationships, deep commitment to each other, and intimate sharing of the life of Jesus are distinctive marks of the Christian church. These marks characterize the church as Jesus intended it to be. Anything less than these characteristics is less than His desire for His body. To further enhance the development and maturity of His body, the Lord of the church gave various ministry gifts to the church through the Holy Spirit to facilitate the mutual sharing of fellowship and nurture.

1-5 Based on the content you have just considered, circle the letter preceding the correct answer for each of the following questions.

1 The primary purpose of Christian sharing groups is to
a) exchange views on the Bible's teachings.
b) become a part of Christ's body.
c) share the life of Christ with others on a more personal level.
d) receive the new life Jesus offers.

2 Christian sharing groups are characterized by the
a) desire to have equal material wealth.
b) commitment of each member to the spiritual welfare of other members.
c) feeling of sympathy each member has for the problems of others.
d) sense of facing the same problems.

3 Relationships within Christian sharing groups provide for the individual participants of the group by
a) helping them to affirm each other and so facilitate spiritual growth.
b) providing a basis for comparing godly living.
c) helping them avoid "worldly" contacts.
d) providing a group to whom each can witness of his faith.

4 The distinctive marks which Jesus intended to characterize His church are
a) sharing intimate fellowship and rich interpersonal relationships.
b) giving away all material possessions and withdrawing from nonspiritual things.
c) living in seclusion from other people and performing many good works.
d) avoiding those who are not Christians and being critical of weaker Christians.

5 Jesus gave the *spiritual ministry gifts* to His church so that
a) every member might have some meaningful task.
b) people might have some means to survive in a wicked world.
c) Christians would be too busy to be concerned about *worldly* things.
d) the mutual sharing of fellowship and nurture might be facilitated.

Sharing Groups in Historical Perspective

Objective 2. *Select statements which identify correctly how small sharing groups have been used throughout the history of Christianity.*

The idea of Christians meeting in small groups to share the life of Jesus is not new. Jesus knew the significance of intimate sharing which accompanies small group experience. From among His many followers, Jesus chose twelve intimate associates, and from them He developed an effective small group. The relationship of Jesus and the Twelve included many of the elements of group dynamics, which modern social scientists have identified as necessary for meaningful group experience. In this group experience, each individual was nurtured toward spiritual maturity. Moreover, the group itself developed and grew stronger in commitment, purpose, and knowledge as the Lord intended. Therefore, Jesus commissioned the Twelve with the ongoing task of preaching the gospel.

These first Christian leaders continued to use this small group strategy in their ministry. The book of Acts reveals the existence of various small groups during this initial period of Christian history. Acts 2:41-42 indicates that the early Christians met together to share in evangelism, teaching, fellowship, worship, and prayer. Other passages in Acts indicate that first century Christians met regularly in the homes of various Christians. These meetings gave them opportunities for intimate sharing, Bible study, and effective prayer concerning their own needs and those of other Christians. We must emphasize that apart from the times when Jerusalem Christians worshiped at the temple, Christians in general, for several centuries, had no public place of worship of their own in which to meet as a collective body. In spite of this difficulty, the various groups communicated and shared the same overall goals as they met in homes (Acts 12:12; Romans 16:5, 23; Colossians 4:15; Philemon 1-4), public auditoriums of schools (Acts 19:9), and in synagogues (Acts 14:1, 3; 17:1, 18:4), as long as they were permitted to do so. Nevertheless, the work of gospel proclamation went forward effectively and overcame all obstacles.

The pattern of small group meetings established in the apostolic period continued for quite some time. During times of official government persecution, small group meetings offered the additional advantage of security. In this setting, new converts learned the basic truths of Christian faith. Many new Christians were converts from pagan religions. They needed a new orientation to life and reality if they were to live the Christian life effectively. Through these group learning experiences, thousands received the teaching they needed to help them understand both Christian responsibilities and privileges and to further their own spiritual development.

Through the centuries of Christian history, small groups meeting together provided opportunities for Christians to fellowship together, nurture each other, and share their common life and experience. Sometimes the vitality of Christian life and ministry were lost to all but a few who met together in such small sharing groups. At other times, small sharing groups have played an important part in bringing spiritual renewal to the Christian church in various places. John Wesley, for example, organized class meetings which were called *societies* as part of his strategy to conserve the fruits of spiritual revival that swept across Great Britain in the eighteenth century. In the early part of the twentieth century, small group meetings were held in Christian homes in widely separated places in the world. In the United States these small group meetings were known as *cottage prayer meetings*. Elsewhere, small groups met on Bible school campuses, in retreat centers, or wherever they could to address themselves to their spiritual needs and especially to surrender themselves more fully to the control of the Holy Spirit. These meetings helped facilitate the development and spread of the holiness and pentecostal movements, which brought renewed emphasis on personal holy living and on the work and ministry of the Holy Spirit in and through the lives of Christians.

In many parts of the world today, small Christian sharing groups exist. Sometimes these groups meet on an informal basis; other groups are structured more formally. Christians from many walks of life, social levels, various doctrinal beliefs, and religious organizations meet together to share in fellowship, worship, Bible study, and prayer. Sometimes these small groups meet in rooms in office buildings or factories during lunch or after working hours. Sometimes they meet in a conference room at a restaurant or hotel. Frequently, they meet in a school classroom and very often they meet in homes. Whether structured loosely and informally or more formally and whether the place be a lunch room, classroom, an office, or a warehouse, the important thing is that these groups meet and share the life of Jesus and are edified.

Some of the largest Christian congregations in the world organize their people into such groups, commonly called cell groups, neighborhood fellowship groups, or some other similar name. The leaders of these large churches rely on these small group meetings to provide the intimate fellowship and personal ministry each Christian needs to encourage his personal spiritual development.

In every period of Christian history, the purpose of these small group meetings has been the same: to share the life of Christ together. Rich spiritual fellowship occurs and individual Christians find their needs met. Moreover, in this context each believer has opportunities to exercise his gifts in serving others in the body of Christ as well as those who are not yet believers.

You will discover, as have Christians since the time of Jesus, that regular participation in small sharing group activity will help your own spiritual growth. You will find your own needs met through such relationships, and you will also find that these relationships provide you with opportunities to contribute to the spiritual nurture of other Christians.

6 Circle the letter preceding each TRUE statement.

a Small group meetings of Christians are a recent innovation.

b Jesus formed the Twelve into a sharing group.

c Small sharing groups were unknown to first century Christians.

d The book of Acts indicates that first century Christians met together regularly in home meetings.

e Thousands of new Christians were oriented to the Christian life in the small group setting in the early centuries of church history.

f Throughout Christian history, small groups have had little to do with the spread of spiritual renewal.

g Small Christian sharing groups are common today in many parts of the world.

h The largest church congregations in the world have found that small groups are unacceptable for their use.

i In every period of Christian history, the purpose of small sharing groups has been to share the life of Christ together.

j Participation in a small sharing group will probably produce little desirable good in your spiritual life.

Meeting Individual Needs in Sharing Groups

Objective 3. *Match four interpersonal needs with the correct sharing group activity which meets each one.*

Psychologists have found that people have certain basic needs: intellectual, social, physical, psychological, and spiritual. For Christians, small sharing groups help in all areas of human need but meet spiritual and relationship needs best. These two go hand-in-hand because the Christ-life is a shared life. All Christians share it together. Let's turn our attention now to an examination of four of the basic needs shared by all people.

1. *Every person needs to belong.* We find our identity and our sense of selfhood by belonging to a group. We develop our sense of self-worth and personal value through interaction with people who accept and love us for Christ's sake. While this kind of relationship is possible in the church, its likelihood is much greater in small groups, where we can get to know others more intimately. A child, for example, develops his personal identity by belonging to his

family. In a similar way, new Christians develop their identity as children of God and members of Christ's body by belonging to a fellowship of other Christians. Everyone needs to be loved, accepted, included, and to belong. Participation in a Christian sharing group provides an opportunity for this need to be met in a meaningful way.

2. *Each of us needs to relate interpersonally with other people.* People in general are social beings. Throughout the world, they either find or create social groupings into which they fit themselves. Few choose to live their lives in isolation. We build communities and cities and we relate ourselves with other people. It is believed that the more complex a society becomes the more interdependent the people become. We need each other and we need to relate on a more personal level with others. We develop best in the impact of our life on another life. The mutual give and take of interpersonal relationships is necessary for healthy personality development. In like fashion, the mutal give and take of interpersonal relationships within the body of Christ is necessary for spiritual growth and development. The help we give and receive fosters growth and development. While it may require some adaptation initially, we need to develop *trust* in those with whom we relate. This will produce real stability and commitment to the group and its ministry within the body of Christ.

3. *Each person has a need to share.* Because we recognize ourselves to be persons of innate worth, we feel a need to share our discoveries, to include others in what we know, think, and feel. Because we belong to each other, we need mutual interaction. We need to receive insights from others and we need to share our insights with significant others who may benefit from the mutual interchange. This need to share derives from our understanding of mutuality, selfhood, and relationship. Because of the work of Jesus within our lives, we gain experience in spiritual growth which will be of value and help to others who encounter similar situations. By sharing our discoveries with others, we grow spiritually and provide them with help which can result in their growth, too.

4. *Every person has a need to participate.* We feel a need to give, to contribute, and to take part in communal affairs. None of us can be truly content simply to receive from others. We need to take part,

to be included, and to help as we can. We need to be a part of what is going on, to be involved, to receive from others, and also to give to them from our resources. Participating in the Christian mission, sharing Jesus with others, helping others develop toward Christlikeness—all these are opportunities for Christians to give active expression to their faith. Opportunities to do this are particularly available through participation in Christian sharing groups.

Small sharing groups, then, provide a setting in which Christians can have these needs met. They also furnish a setting in which Christians can help meet these needs for others in the group. The intimacy and mutuality that develops in such a small group setting makes it possible to extend oneself toward the other participants of the group so that each is mutually helped by the relationship. The purpose of these small groups is to provide the framework in which this can happen. The activities and functions of the group should be structured so that help can be extended to every participant. An atmosphere of love, trust, concern for others, openness regarding one's needs and problems, and a willingness to help in whatever way is necessary is essential in the small sharing group. Characteristically, this is the kind of atmosphere one finds in these group settings.

7 Match each of the four interpersonal needs (right) with the manner in which it is met (left).

....**a** Growth and development are fostered through interaction with other Christians in a loving, caring setting.

....**b** Opportunities for Christians to give expression to their faith come by means of active involvement.

....**c** A sense of identity develops as one becomes part of a fellowship of other Christians.

....**d** Experiences we have can benefit others who encounter similar situations; they are helped and we grow.

1) Need to belong
2) Need to relate interpersonally
3) Need to share
4) Need to participate

Sharing Group Functions

Objective 4. *Identify statements from a list of alternatives which indicate the functions of Christian sharing groups.*

A mature Christian is one who understands his Christian responsibilities and knows how to utilize the resources God has provided to meet them. These responsibilities fall into three groups: 1) to God, 2) to himself, and 3) to others. First, his responsibilities to God include giving God the worship, adoration, and glory due Him. God is unrivalled and He wants us to recognize His worth and give glory to Him. This is done through prayer and communion with Him and by praising Him for what He has done. We also recognize His worth as we learn to depend on Him to meet all our needs and bear our burdens. Second, the responsibilities of the mature Christian to himself include developing a healthy understanding of himself and who he is as God's child, his need for further spiritual growth, and the need to express his faith. A balanced understanding of his strengths and weaknesses is essential. He develops right values and priorities. The nurture of one's own spiritual life is essential in the development of the wholeness we discussed earlier. Third, the mature Christian has responsibilities to others, both other members of the body of Christ and those who have not yet received new life in Christ. These interpersonal responsibilities include receiving support, strength, and help from others and giving the same in return. There is an interdependence between members within the body of Christ.

Properly structured, Christian sharing groups help people develop in each of these three areas of responsibility. The functions of Christian sharing groups include fellowship, Bible study, worship, prayer, and evangelism.

Fellowship is built on mutual caring, a sense of belonging to each other. Those who enjoy fellowship share together out of an awareness that they are vitally joined together by a common life in Christ. This is a major function of Christian sharing groups. They should be places where people who mutually care for each other come together to share joys, disappointments, growth, heartaches, spiritual insights, questions, problems, love, concern, sorrows, and burdens. As these are shared openly, they are mutually borne by the other members of the group. Fellowship involves the exercise of true Christian love and meets the deepest human need: to be surrounded by caring, loving people. Fellowship requires being together and sharing together, and through it spiritual nurture occurs.

Bible study in sharing groups should involve primarily the sharing of Bible truth. This most often takes the form of discussion rather than lecture. Ideally, the group explores Scripture together to discover what God says, what the text meant when it was originally written, and how its truth applies to their own lives to meet their day-to-day needs. Group Bible study need not be viewed as the sharing of uninformed opinions or the sharing of mutual ignorance. Rather, each participant should carefully study the passage under consideration in advance and come to the group meeting with well thought out contributions and questions. Studying the Bible together with the kind of study format we say in Lesson 7 aids spiritual growth. As the shared insights are applied individually and personally, each participant grows from interacting with the Word and with other group members. Moreover, he learns to accept alternate points of view that are equally valid. And with this he develops sensitivity to the feelings of others. Best of all, however, group members learn the teachings of the Word of God and how they apply to life situations.

Worship involves giving honor, respect, or reverence to one who is worthy. In Christian worship we express reverence and honor to God for who He is. This expression may be demonstrated in singing, thanksgiving, praise, prayer, and testimony. Many times reading appropriate Scriptures, singing carefully chosen songs, and making meaningful comments concerning God's character and activity stimulate an awareness of His holy presence and a recognition of His divine love and power. Small group meetings provide a natural setting for such spiritual activities. Often more time can be given to these activities in small group meetings than in regular church services. Worship activities should be a normal part of small group meetings.

Sharing groups provide an excellent setting for sharing burdens and needs in prayer and fulfilling the scriptural command to "carry each other's burdens" (Galatians 6:2). Opportunity should be given for people to relate their problems and needs so other group participants can truly share these burdens and bear them meaningfully to God in prayer. In prayer we commune with God and express our deepest, heartfelt needs to Him. Many different patterns of prayer may be followed in a small group setting. For example, the whole group may pray together, expressing the various needs to God, or one person may lead the group in prayer, expressing the needs and requests of the group. A period of silent prayer will permit everyone to express silently to God what is in his heart. Conversational praying also lends itself to the sharing group setting. Praying together is one of the best and most satisfying ways to carry each other's burdens, and it is one of the essential functions of small group meetings.

Evangelism is presenting the gospel to the unconverted through the power of the Holy Spirit so that they may receive Christ as their personal Savior and follow Him as their Lord. One of the functions of Christian sharing groups is to introduce people to Christ simply, clearly, and persuasively. Someone who is experienced in leading others to Christ should have the opportunity to present the essential truths of the gospel message in small group settings. Group participants often feel free to invite their friends to attend such a meeting. Visitors are often more comfortable attending a small meeting than they would be if they were to attend a regular church service. Group participants should be encouraged to invite their unsaved friends to small group meetings with the assurance that their unsaved friends will be exposed to the clear, meaningful claims of the gospel.

8 Circle the letter preceding each activity in the following list which we discussed as one of the functions of Christian sharing groups.
a) Sharing time together in fellowship
b) Explaining how to receive Christ as Savior
c) Debating a political policy
d) Discussing how to apply a Bible truth to daily life

e) Expressing reverence and honor to God
f) Lecturing for long periods on Bible themes
g) Trading recipes for preparing favorite foods
h) Demonstrating Christian love in sharing others' needs
i) Singing songs which express God's greatness
j) Discussing a current affairs event
k) Praying for the needs of a group member
l) Inviting people to receive Christ as their Savior

IDENTIFYING PRINCIPLES OF GROUP EFFECTIVENESS

Objective 5. *Identify situations which match each of three principles of group effectiveness.*

Dynamic forces are at work whenever two or more individuals work together to achieve a common goal. These forces include such matters as 1) the purpose and background of the group, 2) the personalities and backgrounds of the individuals who make up the group, and 3) the goals of the participants. These are the forces which determine the interaction of the group. Interpersonal relationships, communication patterns, and decision making processes are all affected by group dynamics.

Certain principles result from these dynamics which contribute to group effectiveness. Both group participants and group leaders should be aware of these principles to achieve maximum effectiveness from the group.

The first principle to observe is the principle of *group participation*. All members must be involved in the group process. They must feel free to exchange ideas openly and to share in the group's conclusions and decisions. One person should not dominate the group. Those who tend to dominate group functions should be helped to understand the importance of allowing others to contribute too. Those who tend to be shy, inhibited, and uninvolved should be helped to become active participants in the group's processes.

Another principle of group effectiveness is *group communication*. This involves what is said, how it is said, and the impact it has. Effective communication involves at least three major aspects: 1) the actual verbal message, the words that are spoken; 2) vocal punctuation, the tone in which the words are spoken; and 3) visual punctuation, the nonverbal punctuation, the visual gestures a communicator uses to convey his message. For effective communication to occur, all three of these must be in agreement. To indicate one thing in words and another in the nonverbal ways causes confusion.

In the processes of communication, one aims to convey an idea as he conceives it in his mind. The goal is for others to understand clearly the ideas as he conceived them originally. This calls for effective speaking and listening. In the group process, it is necessary to communicate clearly so that every one can understand what is intended.

EFFECTIVE SPEAKING + EFFECTIVE LISTENING = COMMUNICATION

Still another principle of group effectiveness is *group atmosphere*. This refers to the feelings participants have for each other. Group atmosphere may range from full acceptance on the one hand to defensiveness on the other. For group effectiveness, participants need to feel free to express their true personal feelings without fear of rejection. The group needs to be supportive so that no one is inhibited or threatened by the presence of others. Every member needs to develop flexibility in adjusting to the needs of others and to the different tasks of the group.

9 Match each situation (left) with the appropriate principle of group effectiveness (right).

....**a** One man does all the talking.

....**b** James feels threatened because Pastor John is present.

....**c** A lady gestures with her eyes as she speaks.

....**d** Everyone accepts Paul's insights even though he is unschooled.

....**e** The group leader makes sure that everyone has an opportunity to share his viewpoint.

....**f** The group leader encourages everyone to speak clearly and accurately what he is thinking.

....**g** Narciso hardly listens to what is being said.

....**h** The group leader promotes an open exchange of ideas and feelings.

....**i** Mrs. Gomez is too shy to share her ideas.

1) Group Participation
2) Group Communication
3) Group Atmosphere

LEADING SHARING GROUPS

Objective 6. *Identify common concerns facing those who organize and lead sharing groups.*

Perhaps you have participated in small group activity, either by serving on a committee, attending a class, or perhaps in some informal way. You may have participated in a Christian group similar to what you have read about in this lesson. You may be able to recall situations which illustrate, either positively or negatively, many of the points discussed in this lesson. And it may be that you have been a regular participant in a Christian sharing group. If so, I am sure the experience has had a nurturing affect on your spiritual life. I hope you are developing a growing awareness that God wants you not only to mature spiritually but also to help others grow toward Christlikeness. In helping others grow, you may find yourself organizing and leading sharing groups. The final section of this lesson is designed to answer some of the more common and practical considerations related to this task. We trust you will find the following list helpful as you address yourself to the task of organizing and leading sharing groups.

1. *Where should it meet?* One of the early considerations in organizing a Christian sharing group is where to meet. The only appropriate answer to this is anywhere the group can meet and carry out its purpose. I have met with such groups in restaurants or hotels, in conference rooms in office buildings, and in lunchrooms at factories. Some groups meet in school rooms; however, probably more sharing groups meet in the homes of the participants than in any other place. Generally the home meeting should be encouraged wherever possible. This setting lends an air of informality to the meeting, and participants tend to be more relaxed in this environment than in the more formal setting of an office, hotel, or factory lunch-room. Some groups meet at the same home regularly; other groups meet in turn in the different participants' homes.

2. *When, how often, and for what length of time should it meet?* Another concern that arises is when to meet. The answer to that is whenever it is most convenient for group participants. I have met with such groups for before-breakfast meetings, at lunch time, and in the evening hours. I know of some groups that meet at midmorning or in the late afternoon. The best time for the participants is the right time to meet. The best day of the week is, again, whichever day is most convenient for all concerned. Normally these sharing groups meet about once a week for a one or two hour meeting. However, the frequency and length of the meeting should be based on the needs and desires of the participants and their ability

to come. Flexibility in planning is necessary at all times in sharing group meetings, but this is especially true in the early stages of their development.

3. *Who should participate?* The matter of who participates in such a group may also become a concern. Some groups begin as evangelistic outreaches in which nonbelievers make up the majority of participants. As the gospel begins to work in the lives of these people, many receive new life in Christ and the complexion of the group changes. Some groups are organized for women, while others are for men or for a mixed group of men and women. Some are organized along age lines, such as: 1) teen-age or youth, 2) young adult, 3) middle adult, and 4) senior adult groups. Many groups are formed on the basis of common interests; therefore, those who work in the same office or plant, attend the same school, or, most commonly, live in the same neighborhood or geographical area tend to meet with those who have common points of interest. Christian sharing groups can be organized *anywhere* among *any* group of people which desires Christian fellowship and is willing to commit itself to nurture individual members toward spiritual growth.

4. *What size group is best for optimum results?* Closely related to the goal of nurturing spiritual growth is another vital concern: the size of the group. Some people tend to say, "the more the merrier." This may be true for games and parties, but it does not work well for sharing groups. Let's see why this is true. It is a fact that the larger a group gets the more interpersonal relationships are required of its members. This means that there is less time for interaction with each member, and there are fewer opportunities for truly personal sharing. When sharing groups lose their personal character, they become less meaningful to participants and may be considered as "just another church-related activity." Individuals tend to manage a certain number of interpersonal relationships well. Beyond that number the relationsips are no longer significant; they are only casual and may be forced. Thus, when a group increases beyond a certain size, its efforts become counterproductive. Think about this for a moment.

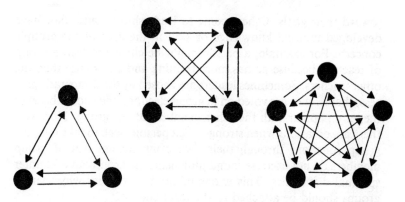

As you can see in the diagram above, a group of three persons involves six interpersonal relationships, a group of four persons involves twelve interpersonal relationships, and a group of five persons involves twenty interpersonal relationships. Obviously, the larger the group the greater the number of relationships each person must develop and maintain. Because of this factor, many experienced group leaders have found that the ideal small group size is about eight-twelve persons; the largest number it can have and still retain its *small group character* is about fifteen persons. Thus, when a group grows to about fifteen persons, it should be reorganized into two smaller groups. When these groups grow to this same size again, another regrouping should take place. Those who work regularly with small group leadership find that smaller groups tend to increase more rapidly than larger groups do. Thus, for optimum results, the small group should include about ten but not more than fifteen people.

5. *Who will lead*? Still another concern of those who wish to organize Christian sharing groups is the matter of leadership. There are different ways in which leaders emerge in a group. Quite frequently, pastors appoint leaders to serve as intitial group leaders. They appoint those who have demonstrated soundness in character, depth of spiritual insight, and sensitivity to the Holy Spirit. Later on, when the group has some experience, some leaders arise because of their charismatic personalities. They seemingly possess qualities which attract others, and they have the ability to inspire others

toward their goals. Others come to leadership because they have developed unusual knowledge or skill in the area of the group's concern. For example, a person might be chosen to lead a group of teachers because he has more training and experience than the other teachers. Sometimes leaders are chosen by the democratic process, that is, they are voted on in group elections and chosen because they are popular with the other members of the group. However, there are occasions when strong-willed persons seek to take over the group functions through their own campaigning. And if group members do not exercise sound judgment, the group can encounter spiritual difficulties. This is one of the best reasons why sharing groups should be attached to the local church.

Ideally, a good leader will be inspiring, have charisma and possess special knowledge and skills. Because of his love for God and other people, others will want to follow him. Also, if his level of spiritual maturity and depth of spiritual insight is greater than that of others, he will be able to help them develop spiritually. Moreover, if he is popular with the group, his chances of being selected for leadership are excellent. You will do well to strive to be the kind of person who can lead others toward spiritual growth.

The leader's task in a Christian sharing group is to guide the group process, to encourage spiritual interaction with God's Word and with each other. The leader may direct the Bible study or give an evangelistic presentation. On some occasions, however, he might sit back and listen or participate in discussion while others teach or guide discussion. The leader's role is to facilitate the group's interaction and to keep its activities and processes directed toward reaching the group's goal. In the case of Christian sharing groups, the goal is to foster the spiritual growth of each participant. The primary reason-for-being of Christian sharing groups is spiritual, rather than social, in nature. This fact must be kept in focus if the group is to achieve its goals.

As noted earlier, another important function of the leader is to harmonize the activities of the group with that of the larger body, the church of which it is part. As with the natural body, the spiritual body is strong and healthy as the members work together, each part functioning according to His design and purpose. As individual groups do the work of the corporate body of Christ, the task of evangelism is accomplished, the fruits of evangelism are conserved, and spiritual growth toward maturity is in evidence. Through sharing groups, individual members of the church have the opportunity to exercise their gifts, help others, and develop Christian maturity. In the context of the larger body, they can receive further encouragement as they recognize the results of their collective efforts, both in their own area and abroad through the foreign missions endeavor. The alert leader will make every effort to keep the activities of the group in proper focus. As a responsible servant of Christ, he will be amenable not only to the Chief Shepherd of the flock but also to the local pastor which the Lord has placed over His flock. He should also recognize any tendency to move away from the nurturing goals of the group and toward personality-centered activities. Sharing groups will play an effective role in the church as long as they are Christ-centered and Christ-exalting. Any group pursuit which aims at less than building His body will fall short of permanent results and overall success.

10 Circle the letter preceding each TRUE statement.

a Sharing groups most frequently meet in settings outside the homes of group members.

b A sharing group should meet at the most convenient time for all members and for as long as and as frequently as is practical.

c The matter of *who should meet* depends in part on the interest of the group.

d Concerning the *size of sharing groups*, a good rule is this: "the more the merrier."

e One of the major factors in determining the optimum size of a sharing group is the number of interpersonal relationships which a person can manage.

f Leadership most generally emerges as a result of one's ability to dominate others, to control their thinking.

261

g The ideal Christian leader will at times direct the activities of the group; at other times he may facilitate the group process as a participant while others lead the activities.

h The alert leader will seek to harmonize the group's activities with those of the larger body, the church, of which it is part.

11 One important reason why leaders must try to harmonize the activities of their groups with those of the larger body, according to our discussion, is that
a) the parent body, the church, may not recognize the group if it doesn't observe all church rules.
b) pastors of churches generally resent any activities that they cannot personally oversee and control, fearing that false doctrine will result.
c) the task of the body is accomplished best as each member does his part.

12 All of the following but one are concerns of sharing group leaders. Which one is NOT stated in the text as a legitimate concern?
a) A group leader should be concerned with the location of group meetings.
b) The group leader must be aware of the most convenient time to meet, the length of each meeting, and the frequency of meetings.
c) The group leader should consider the optimum size of the sharing group.
d) The group leader should be aware of his position of power and use it to accomplish his own program.

self-test

1 Christian sharing groups exist for each of the following purposes but one. Which one is NOT a stated purpose of sharing groups?
a) Sharing groups meet to share the life of Jesus with other Christians.
b) Christian sharing groups have a commitment to the growth and development of group members.
c) The ministry gifts which our Lord gave were meant to facilitate fellowship and nurture.
d) Sharing groups are the primary element in social action and recreation and the means by which we are to change society.

2 The purpose of sharing groups, viewed from the total history of the Christian church, is to
a) provide an alternative to large group meetings, which are less spiritual.
b) enable dissident members of the body of Christ to have a place to express their anxieties and frustrations.
c) share the life of Jesus with other members and stimulate one another to good works, growth, and spiritual development.
d) create a place where spiritual super-saints can be developed in isolation from the rest of the less spiritual members of the body.

3 Sharing groups meet the interpersonal *need to belong* by providing us with
a) significant people who learn to know, love, and accept us for Christ's sake.
b) an organization which has no membership requirements and is committed to self-help.
c) a place where we can sound off against the unfairness of the system of organized religion.
d) other people who share the same problems and want to hear all the common miseries restated by their fellow Christians.

4 The *need to relate interpersonally with other people* is met best, according to this lesson, by Christian sharing groups through the
a) fellowship aspect of relaxed association in which we can hide our problems from other members.
b) interaction provided by other Christians in a loving, caring setting, in which *give and take* growth and development can occur.
c) constant confession of all our sins and faults to others who understand our problems.
d) opportunities one has to meet and interact with others without making any long-term commitment to a formal organization.

5 The *need to share*, we have seen, is met best within the context of sharing groups
a) as individual members release tension by telling their problems.
b) by the spiritual cleansing that takes place in public confession.
c) because of mutuality, selfhood, and relationship: we help others and grow in maturity in the process.
d) because in small group settings each member has an opportunity to bare his soul before others and get a group analysis of his problems and effective cures prescribed as well.

6 People's *need to participate* is met especially by sharing groups because
a) members are forced to be a part of group activities, regardless of their feelings.
b) the nature of sharing groups enables individuals to be involved in both giving to and receiving from other members.
c) the structure of the group is such that all members must at times be leaders.
d) in order to function effectively, each member must seek a dominant role.

7 We have learned that one principle of group effectiveness, *group participation*, is important to the functioning of the group process because
a) the group can only meet individuals' needs as members exchange ideas freely and share in group conclusions and decisions.
b) without 100 percent participation of members on all issues no solutions can be reached.

c) it always produces a healthy consensus, which is good for the group.
d) it keeps all members happy and guarantees a successful outcome.

8 A second important principle of group effectiveness, according to this lesson, is *group communication*. It is important because communication
a) is the only major problem which prevents members from receiving help.
b) is thought to be central to group understanding without which the work of the group is ineffective.
c) involves what is said, how it is said, and the impact it has.
d) is the lifeline of the group in its relationship with the parent church body.

9 *Group atmosphere*, a third important principle of group effectiveness, according to our study, is important to the group process because it determines the
a) degree of acceptance members have for one another.
b) attitude members bring to group meetings.
c) degree of commitment each member will have to the group.
d) basic attitudes that will prevail throughout the life of the group.

10 All of the following are practical aspects involved in organizing and leading Christian sharing groups but one. Which statement is NOT one of the aspects we considered in this lesson?
a) Where the group should meet and how it should relate to the larger body is an important consideration.
b) When, how frequently, and for how long are matters of great importance to group organizers.
c) Who should participate and what size of group is most effective are two important matters to group leaders.
d) The kind of social entertainment and recreational activities and how they can complement the fellowship, study, and worship aspects of the group process are significant leadership issues.

answers to study questions

7 a 2) Need to relate interpersonally.
  b 4) Need to participate.
  c 1) Need to belong.
  d 3) Need to share.

1 c) share the life of Christ.

8 You should have circled a), b), d), e), h), i), k), and l).

2 b) commitment of each member.

9 a 1) Group participation.
  b 3) Group atmosphere.
  c 2) Group communication.
  d 3) Group atmosphere.
  e 1) Group participation.
  f 2) Group communication.
  g 2) Group communication.
  h 3) Group atmosphere.
  i 1) Group participation.

3 a) helping them to affirm each other.

10 a False.
  b True.
  c True.
  d False.
  e True.
  f False.
  g True.
  h True.

4 a) sharing intimate fellowship.

11 c) the task of the body is accomplished.

5 d) the mutual sharing of fellowhip and nurture might be facilitated.

12 d) The group leader should be aware of his position of power.

6 a False.
   b True.
   c False.
   d True.
   e True.
   f False.
   g True.
   h False.
   i True.
   j False.

LESSON 10

Growing in Churches

Juan and Maria sought to make their home the ideal place in which Manuel could grow to maturity. They wanted him to have happy, memorable growing-up experiences. They knew that one day their son must accept the responsibilities of an adult. The time would come when he would choose a vocation, select a marriage partner, rear children, and become active in community affairs. They were delighted that his growth and development involved healthy activities and interests which would reflect more mature behavior.

In a similar way, our heavenly Father wants His children to identify with a fellowship of believers, the church, so that they can be nurtured toward spiritual maturity and be equipped for active involvement in Christian service. Churches provide both training for Christian growth and maturity and equipping for ministry.

In the final lesson of this course, you will study an overview of the church's nurturing ministry. As you study this lesson, you will discover how fellowship with a church can help you grow toward spiritual maturity and how it will help equip you to assist others in growing spiritually.

lesson outline

The Church: A Place for Nurture
The Development of Ministry Structures
The Training for Ministry
The Personnel for Nurturing Ministries

lesson objectives

When you finish this lesson you should be able to:

■ Explain what churches do to facilitate spiritual growth toward Christlikeness.

■ Describe three principles of local church nurturing ministries.

■ Explain the biblical concept of ministry and how it relates to the task of equipping all Christians for Christian service.

■ Discuss the roles of pastors and teachers in the nurturing ministries of the church.

learning activities

1. Work through the lesson development according to the usual procedure. After you have completed the lesson, take the self-test and check your answers.

2. Carefully review Unit 3 (Lessons 8-10), especially the lesson objectives and self-tests. Then complete the unit student report for Unit 3 and send it to your instructor.

key words

accountability	credibility	prospective
affiliation	implement	visually
aptitude	(verb)	vocations
artificial	inadequacy	volitional
competent	misconception	

lesson development

THE CHURCH: A PLACE FOR NURTURE

Objective 1. *Identify statements which describe how the Christian life is nurtured through the ministry of local churches.*

In the broadest sense, the church includes all believers who have received new life in Jesus. When you were *born again*, you received Jesus' life and were spiritually joined to Him and to all others who share His life. You thus became a part of a spiritual body, the church. When we refer to the church in the New Testament sense, we think of those who have been called together to follow Jesus. This body of Christ's followers is referred to correctly as the church.

There are two aspects of Christ's church: the universal and the local. The universal aspect refers to the term *church* in the broad sense. It is composed of all who share the life of Jesus by virture of the new birth. It is universal because it includes all Christian believers from all places throughout church history. The local church refers to the local assembly or congregation. The local church is the manifestation of the universal church in a particular place. Without the local church, the universal church could have no specific expression. Thus, the local church is the fellowship of redeemed people who unite themselves together in a given place to carry out the purposes and mission of the universal church. It is the body of Christ in a specific place.

Christ, the Head of the church, expresses Himself on earth through the church. The mission of the church is thus an extension of the mission of Jesus. He has challenged the church to continue the work He began (Matthew 28:19-20; Mark 16:15; Luke 24:46-49). Local churches as part of the universal church, share responsibility for accomplishing this mission. Every believer is a part of it and has a part to play in it! People who are joined to Christ by the new birth should be brought into His body by their affiliation with a local congregation of believers. Here their spiritual life can be nurtured toward Christlikeness and they find opportunities to contribute to the spiritual development of other Christians. These two ideas can be summed up by saying, "Churches are places where Christian nurture should take place."

This brief introduction to the nature of the church calls attention to two major facts: 1) every Christian is a part of the universal body of Christ and should therefore identify with the life, witness, and fellowship of a local body of believers, and 2) Christ's mission is also our mission. His purpose is to redeem from every people a body of believers and transform them into His own likeness. As part of His body, we have been challenged to carry out His mission. We can be more effective in this mission as we grow in the knowledge of His Word and use the spiritual gifts He has given. Spiritual growth, which involves insight into the application of God's Word to everyday situations, also comes about through witnessing to unbelievers and sharing with those less mature than ourselves. To be as effective as possible in Christ's work, we need to grow toward spiritual maturity.

271

Some of the material you have studied in this course pertains more to the universal aspect of the church, but this lesson focuses on the local expression of the church. Part of the task of local churches is to nurture spiritual life toward maturity. In and through the ministry of the local church, you will find the help you need to grow spiritually. You will also find abundant opportunities to help others mature toward Christlikeness.

As the people of God in the local church work together harmoniously, the growth needs of the body are met and the unconverted are attracted to Christ. Moreover, the believers who make up the body of Christ are nurtured and equipped for meaningful involvement in serving others.

The ministry of God's Word in churches serves two essential purposes: 1) it calls the unconverted to faith in Christ, and 2) it nurtures the faith of believers, teaching them to live lives that please and glorify God. While this ministry may express itself in many forms, such as teaching, encouraging, admonishing, and correcting, its purposes remain the same. In the matter of nurturing the spiritual life of believers, two concerns come into focus: 1) training for maturity, and 2) equipping for involvement in service. These are the results of the church's ministry of God's Word.

Everyone recognizes that instruction and training are a vital part of helping a child grow to maturity. A child must be taught to clothe and feed himself, to read, to relate properly to others, and to control his emotions, among other important responsibilities. Parents and teachers cooperate to help children make these changes. In a similar way, the church offers ministry opportunities which are designed to provide spiritual growth and development toward spiritual maturity.

From a biblical point of view, the ultimate goal of spiritual growth is Christlikeness. As we grow spiritually, we move progressively toward spiritual maturity. One measure of expression of spiritual maturity is Christian service. Our desire to be Christlike will lead us to serve as He served and to be involved in the spiritual development of others. Another expression of Christian maturity is the development of sound spiritual insight, judgment, and character.

At this point review what you studied in Lesson 2 in the section entitled *Six Need Levels*. Carefully observe the progression from spiritual infancy toward spiritual maturity. Notice, also, that the development is toward involvement in Christian service. Christian life is more than *hearing*, it is also *doing* (James 1:22). Ephesians 4:11-16 indicates that all of God's people are to do works of Christian service. These verses also teach that church leaders are to equip God's people to do their service for Him. In addition, verse 16 suggests that a Christian demonstrates his maturity in Christ by properly taking his place in the body of Christ, drawing strength from the body, and giving his strengths and gifts to the welfare and development of others. Thus, the body of Christ develops and matures as each member performs his service. This is accomplished as the church, through its members and leaders, nurtures the spiritual lives of its members and equips them for effective Christian service. The church, through its nurturing ministry, informs its members of their responsibilities, encourages them to use their skills and talents for God's glory, and provides opportunities for service.

1 Circle the letter in front of each TRUE statement.

a A local church is the manifestation of Christ's universal body in a particular place.

b Christ's universal body consists of mature Christians and differs from a local congregation of believers whose members are essentially immature.

c Whether a Christian should identify with a local church or not is a matter of preference, since the Bible is silent on this matter.

d Since every Christian is part of the universal church, he should affiliate with a local body of believers.

e The ministry of the local church is geared primarily toward evangelism and has little concern with helping converts grow toward spiritual maturity.

f Growing Christians can expect to find the help they need to grow spiritually in the ministry of the local church.

g The local church is a place where maturing Christians can learn about their responsibilities and be equipped to render Christian service.

h Growth toward spiritual maturity seldom expresses itself in observable ways.

i The ultimate goal of spiritual growth is Christlikeness in which the believer is equipped for involvement in service for Christ.

j As a local church exercises its God-given ministries, individual believers are nurtured toward spiritual growth and equipped for effective Christian service.

THE DEVELOPMENT OF MINISTRY STRUCTURES

Objective 2. *Distinguish between examples of appropriate and inappropriate structures for ministry and correct and incorrect reasons for their existence.*

To help promote their evangelism and outreach services, local churches develop ministry programs. These programs are based on Christian service principles like those you have studied in this course. The programs local churches develop are an attempt to put Christian beliefs into practice in ways that will achieve their ministry goals.

In the attempt to build meaningful ministry programs, local churches seek to meet the spiritual development needs of all persons, regardless of their stage of spiritual development or age level. In providing opportunities for service, local churches enable maturing believers to apply what they have learned in helping others. This ministry outlet supplies help for new believers and exercise for the emerging talents and skills of developing believers, as well as growth in Christlikeness and Christian maturity. Because of the varied needs of new and mature Christians, local churches seek to offer programs that are balanced, graded, and organized.

A local church's nurturing ministry is balanced when it offers the full range of opportunities needed to assist people in developing spiritually in every area of their lives. The New Testament church emphasized evangelism, teaching, fellowship, worship, and prayer (Acts 2:41-42). All of these activities are essential to full spiritual development. Thus, local churches should examine their ministry programs to ensure that they are offering balanced opportunities in each of these five areas. A local church should design activities which address each of these ministry areas. It should also offer a balanced program that will provide opportunities for everyone in the fellowship to take advantage of these services.

2 In your notebook prepare a chart similar to the following example. Down the left side of the page, list all of the ministry programs your local church sponsors. Then make a check in the column which shows best the major ministry emphasis of each program. Once this is complete, analyze it to discover if there is a balance in each of these needed ministry areas. You may wish to make about four of these charts: one for the early childhood age level, one for the middle childhood level, one for youth, and one for adults. This exercise will help you to see whether a balanced ministry program is offered at each age level in your church. (NOTE: While the ideal is for each church to have all the structures that are needed to promote total spiritual development, quite frequently churches lack the personnel to initiate graded programs completely. Smaller churches, in fact, may combine programs because of the personnel problem. In any case, we must always use wisdom in our approach to church leaders concerning their method of operation, lest we make them feel that we are criticizing their efforts. In time, perhaps, we can implement these suggestions in our own ministries. Meanwhile, let's not let our zeal for knowledge and effective nurturing programs blind us to the need for charity in our relationship with other Christian workers.)

Ministry Programs	Evangelism	Teaching	Fellowship	Worship	Prayer

Since congregations are made up of a full range of people, from small children to aged adults, a balanced program should include ministry which addresses all five of these areas for all ages. This brings us to the need for a graded program. That training should be graded is a well-understood fact. School children, for example, are graded because of their ages and learning differences. College students are graded on the basis of their previous learning experience and achievements. Churches, operating on the same principle, offer learning opportunities for children, others for youth, and still others for adults. Also, some churches find it necessary to group their learners in other ways to accommodate different levels of academic achievement, interest concerns, and stages of spiritual development. Obviously, the needs of two young men, one a college graduate from a large metropolitan city and the other a farmer with little formal schooling and no experience outside his remote rural village, will be very different. These differences will affect their learning experience. Likewise, two adults who are of similar age may have very different family situations. If the one were married and had children at a rather young age, he might be involved in parent-teen relations. The other person of the same age, however, might be involved in rearing infants or very small children. Their needs and interests, therefore, would be different. To meet the needs of all of its members, a church should structure learning opportunities on a graded basis. A graded program, then, refers to the development of a program of educational opportunities for groups of learners who have similar characteristics that will affect their learning. Graded programs have been found to promote effective learning; therefore, to help its members learn and grow toward spiritual maturity, a church should develop graded programs.

3 Examine the educational program of the local church you attend. Discover how it is graded. Examine it carefully enough to learn if the grading structure is followed and what the basis is for grading. Do needs exist that are not being met which could be solved by a better grading system? What do you find that you consider to be helpful? In what areas might you recommend that changes be made? Write your observations and responses in your notebook, keeping in mind the things we referred to in the NOTE on question 2.

4 Suppose you were to visit a church in a certain city on a Sunday morning. As you enter the sanctuary during the Bible study period, you see that the session includes the entire congregation: children, young people, and adults. You observe a leader who stands in front and teaches. During the period, you notice parents quieting their children, teenagers whispering occasionally, and some adults looking about with disinterest. The teacher pauses occasionally in his lecture to pose questions. Some adults are involved in the discussion which surrounds these questions. In your notebook, explain what you would suggest to 1) involve more people, 2) create interest, 3) solve discipline problems, and 4) promote healthy learning situations for the people of this congregation.

A program that has many activities and features needs to be organized. Research indicates that large tasks can be accomplished best when they are divided systematically into a number of smaller tasks. This is the nature of organization. Organization aids efficiency by grouping similar tasks together and putting each task under the supervision of an individual who can specialize in one aspect of the total work. An organizational system provides the framework within which activities can occur. It connects the various parts of a program into a unified whole and provides coordination of the various parts. An organizational plan also provides communication between the different groups and their leaders and defines the relationships between the parts. Moreover, it establishes the scope of responsibilities and the patterns of authority and accountability.

Churches, whose nurturing programs include a variety of activities, need to organize their efforts to ensure that they achieve the things they want to accomplish: that their programs achieve their intended goals. They also need to organize to help avoid unnecessary overlap in important areas.

Organizational patterns are generally shown on flow charts which show visually how communications flow both vertically and horizontally. Flow charts also show in visual form how a given task relates to the total program and who the supervisors and subordinates are. In a flow chart, the highest levels of responsibility and account-ability are shown at the top of the chart and other activities are shown on respective levels downward. Here is an example of a typical flow chart for a church:

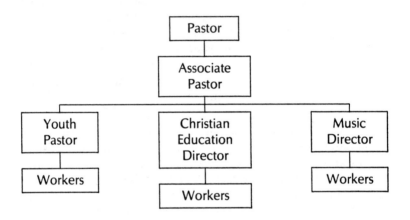

Organizational flow charts are structured by grouping similar tasks together. In church nurturing programs, organizations are generally structured either by similarity of ministry or by age level. In the first, *similarity of ministry structure*, one supervisor oversees the total work of a particular program, such as the church school, children's church, or vacation Bible school. In the *age level structure* all ministry activities are grouped together for a particular age level. Each of these levels is under the leadership of a person who supervises the ministry to that age group. Both of these systems are used by local churches.

5 Examine the organizational structure of your local church. You may need to discuss this with the pastor or some other church leader or administrator. If the church has already developed an organizational flow chart for its nurturing programs, study this chart carefully. If none has been developed, prepare one in your notebook that would be suitable for this particular church.

6 Local churches, according to this study, develop ministry programs in order to promote their
a) status and credibility in their respective communities.
b) outreach and nurturing services.
c) personnel development and increase their attendance.

7 A local church's nurturing ministry is balanced, according to our discussion, when it
a) meets the emotional, intellectual, and volitional needs of people.
b) satisfies the majority of the people involved.
c) offers the opportunities necessary to assist people in developing spiritually in every area of their lives.

8 Graded programs are developed, we have seen, because
a) of the need to distribute the number of people into roughly equal classes so that teachers can manage learners better.
b) groups of learners who have similar learning characteristics learn more effectively than they would in a setting with those of different learning characteristics.
c) there is a need to group all people neatly by age, social status, education, sex, and degree of spiritual maturity.

9 Organizations are structured by grouping similar tasks together. In church nurturing programs, organizations are generally structured by
a) similarity of ministry or age level.
b) aptitude or interests.
c) spiritual development characteristics or vocations.

The local assembly, then, makes possible the nurturing ministries of the church on a broad basis. Through its organizational structures, the local church can minister to the general growth needs of many believers in an efficient, meaningful way. By contrast, the small sharing group can meet the needs of people of a given age, interest, job, or educational group in a very personal and informal way. Each ministry is complementary to the other.

THE TRAINING FOR MINISTRY

Objective 3. *Identify biblical principles of training used in the development of Christian ministries.*

Leadership training is a vital part of a local church's nurturing ministry. You have already discovered that every Christian is to be actively involved in Christian service. In the New Testament, the words *service* and *ministry* come from the same Greek word and carry the same meaning. It is unfortunate, indeed, that in the course of church history an artificial distinction has been drawn between *ministers* and *laymen* in the church. The misconception that only ordained church leaders are ministers is common, but this idea is foreign to the New Testament. According to the Scriptures, every believer is responsible to render Christian service.

God has placed certain leaders in His church and has given them the particular responsibility to train and equip the rest of the body for service. This is the clear teaching of Ephesians 4:11-12. The saints, all the people of God, are to do works of ministry, while the apostles, prophets, evangelists, and pastor-teachers are to prepare (train or equip) the saints to minister.

You may have experienced some degree of fear or feeling of inadequacy the first time you were introduced to this idea. Many Christians experience such feelings. What you experienced was an awareness of your need for training. You felt inadequate and poorly equipped for such a task. This is why God provided leaders to help you. As you receive the instruction of more mature church leaders, you develop a desire to serve Christ and to help others come to Him and mature into His likeness.

God has taken care of the initial equipping of every Christian for ministry. Through the Holy Spirit He has given every member of the church the essential equipment for works of service. The presence of the Holy Spirit in the church and in the believer's life empowers both for effective life and service. In addition, God has given every believer some spiritual gift (or gifts) to equip him for ministry within the body of Christ. Four New Testament passages

280

indicate that every Christian has received such enablement for service: Romans 12:3-8; 1 Corinthians 12:1-11; Ephesians 4:11-16; and 1 Peter 4:10-11. While all members receive a gift or gifts, they do not all receive the same gifts. A variety of gifts has been distributed among the members of the body. Each gift complements the others. As all of them are exercised, the body is made complete.

A major part of the church's responsibility in training its members for ministry involves helping people discover their gift(s). If a Christian is unaware of his gift, how can he be helped to discover what God wants him to do? A good beginning point is the desire to work for the Lord, to be fascinated with a certain aspect of service, to feel attracted or drawn to it. Sometimes this begins as one identifies with or experiences a sense of fulfillment as he watches others serve the Lord in some capacity. Once a person feels drawn to a particular aspect of Christian service, he should look for opportunities to be involved in it. He should experience a sense of fulfillment and satisfaction as he performs this service, if it is truly God's gift to him. In this process, Christians should also discover that God has not called them to certain tasks. This is a wholesome discovery. Perhaps one of the best indicators of a Christian's gift of service is the recognition given to it by more mature believers. As they witness the use of the gift, the spirit in which it is used, and the spiritual response that follows, they can often discern whether this is the beginning of a Spirit-anointed ministry or not. The Spirit within them bears witness to the genuineness of the gift. They can then encourage the individual to continue to develop the gift just as Paul encouraged Timothy (2 Timothy 1:6). A major part of training Christians for ministry, then, is helping them discover the gift God has given them.

It is not enough to discover one's gift. Gifts come packaged in underdeveloped forms. They must be developed through practice and use. Even the most talented musicians find it necessary to practice long and hard hours to develop their potential gifts. This is why the church is involved in the nurturing ministry. Church leaders devote much of their time and energy to the task of training church members for spiritual service. By helping people develop the gifts God has given them, the church, through its leaders, trains Christians for ministry. It also provides opportunities for the application of the lessons learned.

10 Circle the letter in front of each statement which expresses a biblical principle of training for Christian ministries.
a) The only leaders which are to be separated by the church for ministry are apostles, prophets, evangelists, and pastor-teachers.
b) Every believer is responsible to render Christian service.
c) God has placed certain leaders in the church to train and equip members of the body of Christ for ministry.
d) The difference between spiritual leaders and other members of the body permits us to recognize who is most important in God's program.
e) The care God has taken to equip each Christian for effective life and service through the indwelling presence of the Holy Spirit demonstrates His desire for productive Christian ministry.
f) As each member exercises his spiritual gift(s), the body of Christ is edified, for the gifts complement each other and minister to the total needs of the body of Christ.
g) One should develop his gift in private and only use it in public when it can function perfectly.
h) Spiritual leaders can help individuals exercise their gifts by speaking words of encouragement.

THE PERSONNEL FOR NURTURING MINISTRIES

Objective 4. *Demonstrate knowledge of the respective roles of pastors and teachers by differentiating between tasks that belong exclusively to each, both, and to all Christians.*

For a local church to succeed in its nurturing ministry, it must have the leadership of competent and dedicated people. Each group within the program needs a dedicated leader. Therefore, each local church requires a number of people to staff its nurturing programs. Two particular classes of church nurturing leaders are mentioned

In the Bible: 1) pastors and 2) teachers. Without minimizing the importance of other people, we will consider the roles of these two groups which are mentioned in the Scriptures.

Pastors are God's special ministry gift to the church. Generally they have received special training to prepare them for their work. Often they commit all or a majority of their time to the church's ministry. They are responsible for the spiritual leadership of all aspects of the church's work. This includes both general and specific responsibilities for the church's nurturing ministry.

As you read Ephesians 4:11-12 carefully once again, you will observe that pastors and teachers are closely related. In the original language of the New Testament (Greek), the grammar of the passage suggests that these two functions could be combined in the same person. These roles represent two different but interrelated functions which were fulfilled in the church by the same persons. Because of this close relationship, this term is sometimes written *pastors-teachers* to show their close association.

The pastoral function refers to the task of caring for the flock. It is compared to a shepherd who watches and cares for a flock of sheep. The teaching function involves nurturing, training, and developing the people to whom he ministers. The two ideas are really not far apart. The shepherd leads the sheep into pastures where there is an abundance of good food and cool water. The teacher instructs in the Word of God, which is spiritual food, and points people to Jesus, who is the water of life. The pastor-teacher is responsible to watch over and care for the congregation and to teach and train the members for effective service and ultimate maturity. Teaching is an essential part of the pastoral office.

Christians look to their pastor for teaching. They should receive and value his counsel and instructions. Many of his sermons will be instructive. Since he spends much of his time preparing to teach the people, they should respect and protect his study time. This is a very important part of his work and ministry.

The pastor's work involves the oversight of all ministries of the church. One of the general areas under his oversight is that of the nurturing program. He may delegate the specific supervision of the various parts of the program to others, but he gives guidance to the general direction of all ministry programs. In this role, he should function as the main teacher among a team of fellow teachers. In this capacity, he will give oversight to the total nurturing program, and on many occasions he will teach.

According to the passage in Ephesians, pastors are given the very specific responsibility of teaching to prepare God's people for works of service. They are particularly responsible to equip others so that the body of Christ may be built up in knowledge, unity in the faith, and maturity in Christ. Leadership training and ministry development are an important part of the pastor's total responsibility for the church's ministry. He should function as the senior minister in a body of ministers. His particular task is to recognize and develop leadership potential and to train and equip the people of God to minister. This task includes helping people to discover places of service where they can develop and exercise their gifts for God's glory and the upbuilding of the body. In fact, this is a pastor's most challenging task. To develop human potential under God and to equip people for involvement in Christian service is both an awesome responsibility and a great opportunity. Jesus selected special ones from the masses of people who followed Him. From the multitudes He chose to train the Twelve. Paul likewise selected special persons that he could train for leadership in the ministry. Timothy is a prime example of this pattern. This is the specific task of the pastor-teacher.

11 If a pastor's time was very limited and he had to do one of the following and neglect the other, which one, in your opinion, should he do? Circle the letter in each set which indicates your choice. He should:

a) go to a new area to evangelize.
b) teach a group of people how to evangelize.

c) personally make all the sick calls.
d) prepare workers for the ministry of visitation.

e) teach a class for prospective teachers.
f) write an article for a local newspaper.

g) pioneer a church in a nearby village.
h) train some laymen to pioneer churches.

i) get involved in personal evangelism.
j) train five people to get involved in personal evangelism.

k) develop the Christian nurturing program so that the many new people can be grounded solidly in the faith.
l) work extensively on plans for a new church building.

While the pastor is the main teacher of the church, he should not be the only teacher. The varied aspects of the nurturing program require that many people assume teaching responsibilities, and God has prepared for this need by giving teachers to the church. Local churches should make every effort to select those to teach whom God has gifted to be teachers. Teaching is an important ministry that carries great responsibility (James 3:1). Teachers should recognize the importance of their task, for they have a great opportunity to influence the eternal destiny of many people.

Many of the people who teach in the church's nurturing programs will not have the formal educational training which is usual for teachers in public schools. Nor does it seem necessary for them to have such training; however, they do need the qualifications necessary to communicate the truth effectively to their students. Since a major part of teaching in the church is helping people to grow spiritually, church teachers must be alive and growing Christians themselves who know the teachings of Scripture. In addition to their new birth experience, they must have a dynamic, growing relationship with Him and be filled with the Holy Spirit. Their behavior should reflect the quality of life Jesus offers, for they are to be models of the Christ-life.

Dedicated teachers are characterized by their response to the biblical exhortations to grow in grace (2 Peter 3:18) and to develop facility in communicating gospel truth (2 Timothy 2:15). They have keen and growing appetites for the Word of God and Christian ministry. This does not mean that church teachers must know all there is to know in these areas. Probably no one does know all that can be known. It does mean that they should have mastered certain basic biblical teachings. It also means that they should be developing critical insights into the teachings of God's Word and their applications in one's daily life. Moreover, these church teachers should have some understanding of human nature and of the psychological makeup of their pupils. They should also understand certain basic facts concerning the teaching-learning process and how to apply their knowledge in teaching situations. Paul taught Timothy that Christian workers should be faithful persons who should have the ability to teach others (2 Timothy 2:2).

Perhaps you are considering a teaching ministry in your local church. You may feel that God has given you a teaching gift. If so, you should seek to develop and exercise that gift whenever the opportunity presents itself. You can prepare yourself for more effective service by seeking to learn more in the areas we discussed in the foregoing paragraph. I have sought to suggest in this course many of the things that have helped others develop the skills and knowledge necessary to become productive in the nurturing ministry. I trust that these suggestions will give direction to your efforts now and increasingly in the future as you continue to develop your God-given talents.

The very fact that you have completed this course indicates that you have acquired many of the basic skills needed for this sacred and exciting ministry. I now encourage you to use what you have learned. In doing so, you will grow spiritually and you will help others grow toward Christlikeness too.

12 In the following exercise match the appropriate ministry role exercised (right) with the function described (left), based upon the discussion in this section.

....**a** Responsible for the spiritual leadership of all aspects of the church's work and ministry

....**b** Responsible for a segment of the maturing ministry in which members of the body are equipped for service

....**c** Seek to develop human potential under God and equip people for involvement in ministry

....**d** Responsible for the extension of the gospel into all the world through the ministry of the body of Christ.

....**e** The senior minister in a body of ministers

1) Pastors
2) Teachers
3) Both pastors and teachers
4) Christians in general

self-test

TRUE-FALSE. Place a **T** in the blank space in front of each TRUE statement and an **F** in front of each FALSE statement.

.... **1** To have a balanced nurturing ministry, a church must help people develop spiritually in every area of their lives through evangelism, teaching, fellowship, worship, and prayer.

.... **2** It has been found that graded programs demand so many teachers that they are impractical for most churches.

.... **3** A graded program is one that develops educational opportunities for groups of learners who have similar characteristics that affect their learning.

.... **4** Organizational flow charts for churches are structured either by similarity of ministry or age level.

.... **5** Only ordained church leaders are ministers in the New Testament concept of the Greek word translated *service* or *ministry*.

.... **6** If an immature Christian cannot tell what his gift(s) to the church is, he should check his interests, spiritual burdens, and what he gets personal joy and satisfaction from as he works for the Lord for an indication of his gift(s).

.... **7** As Christians mature they will discover not only their gift(s) to the church, but they will also find that there are some tasks God has not called them to do.

.... **8** It is not necessary for a pastor to also be a teacher if he makes sure he has good teachers on his church staff.

.... **9** One of the pastor's tasks is to recognize and develop leadership potential by helping people discover places of service where they can develop and exercise their spiritual gift(s).

....**10** The basic qualification for a teacher in the church's nurturing program should be formal educational training.

Be sure to complete your unit student report for Unit 3 and return the answer sheet to your ICI instructor.

answers to study questions

7 c) offers the opportunities necessary to assist people.

1 a True.
 b False.
 c False.
 d True.
 e False.
 f True.
 g True.
 h False.
 i True.
 j True.

8 b) groups of learners who have similar learning characteristics.

2 Your answer.

9 a) similarity of ministry or age level.

3 Your answer.

10 You should have circled b), c), e), f), and h).

4 Your answer may differ from mine, but they should include principles we've discussed in this course. First, to involve more people we could break up the body into groups graded according to age, interests, and spiritual needs. Second, by moving to a graded system we would undoubtedly do much to create interest, especially if teachers resolved to involve learners in learning activities and guide their discovery. The third problem, discipline, would doubtless be solved to a large degree by the grading of learners into classes with members of their own peer groups. With proper involvement in the teaching-learning situation, much, if not all, of the restlessness and disinterest shown in the single group would disappear. Finally, with learner involvement and guided discovery the environment is right for healthy learning to take place. Here, too, application of lessons learned can be stressed.

11 You should have circled b), d), e), h), j), and k).

5 Your answer.

12 a 1) Pastors.
   b 2) Teachers.
   c 3) Both pastors and teachers.
   d 4) Christians in general.
   e 1) Pastors.

6 b) outreach and nurturing services.

Glossary

The right-hand column lists the lesson in the independent-study textbook in which the word is first used.

		Lesson
abstractions	— expressing or naming qualities or ideas rather than a particular, concrete thing	5
accountability	— being responsible	10
acquisition	— act of acquiring or gaining something	4
adherent	— a faithful supporter or follower	3
admonished	— advised against something; warned	1
admonition	— gentle reproof or warning	8
adversity	— condition of being in unfavorable circumstances	1
affiliation	— joined in close association	10
affinity	— A natural attraction to a person or liking for a thing	6
affirm	— to state positively	9
amenable	— open to suggestion, influence, advice; responsive; submissive	9
aptitude	— natural capacity; talent	10
artificial	— produced by human skill or labor; not natural	10
assimilate	— take in and make part of oneself	4

assumption	— taken for granted without actual proof	6

bereaved	— left desolate and alone (usually because of death)	1
boredom	— weariness caused by dull, tiresome people or things	1

capabilities	— abilities that are learned; potential uses	2
characteristics	— that which distinguishes from others; special; distinctive	1
charismatic	— capable of inspiring great personal allegiance	9
commonalty	— the common people; people as a group	6
compatible	— able to exist or get on well together	1
competency	— properly qualified; able	6
competent	— having adequate ability or qualities	10
competitive	— effort to obtain something wanted by others; rivalry	5
complement	— something that completes or makes perfect	8
compliance	— doing as another wishes; yielding to a request or command	6
concepts	— ideas of a class of objects; general notion	2

conditioning	— act of putting in good condition; state in which a person or thing is	4
conform	— act according to law or rule or standard of conduct expected	2
consistency	— a keeping to the same principles, course of action	6
contentious	— fond of arguing	1
context	— parts directly before and after a word, sentence, etc. that influence its meaning	6
convictions	— firm beliefs; certainties	4
corporate	— united; combined	1
counterpart	— person or thing closely resembling another	1
credibility	— fact or quality of being believable	10
criteria	— rule or standard for making a judgment	7
degeneration	— process of deterioration; growing worse	1
developmental	— process of developing; growth	2
disclosure	— a thing opened to view; uncovered	1
discrepancy	— lack of consistency; difference	6
discriminate	— make or see a difference	1
distinctive	— distinguishing from others; special	2

distorted	— pulled or twisted out of shape	2
domineering	— ruling or governing arbitrarily; asserting one's authority or opinion in an overbearing way	6
durability	— lasting quality; ability to withstand wear	1
dynamically	— having to do with energy; energetic or active	9
edification	— to have moral improvement; spiritual benefit	2
emaciated	— made unnaturally thin; caused to lose flesh or to waste away	1
emulate	— strive to equal or excel	3
encounter	— meet unexpectedly	7
endearing	— inspiring or creating affection for	8
enthralled	— held captive by beauty or interest	1
ethical	— having to do with standards of right and wrong	2
exemplary	— worth imitating; serving as a model	2
expertise	— expert knowledge or opinion	3
explicitly	— clearly expressed; distinctly stated	1
facilitate	— make easy; lessen the labor of	1

familiarity	— close acquaintance; knowledge; intimacy	8
fascination	— attracted to strongly; enchanted by charming qualities	5
generalizations	— general rules, statements inferred from particular facts	4
gratifying	— giving pleasure to; pleasing	8
group dynamics	— the interacting forces within a small group	9
heresy	— a religious doctrine or opinion rejected by the authorities of a church as contrary to the beliefs of that church	7
hierarchy	— organization of persons or things arranged one above the other according to rank, class, or grade	3
hygiene	— science that deals with the maintenance of health	5
identification	— recognition as a particular person or thing	3
imbibe	— drink in; absorb	3
imitation	— thing that tries to be like or act like something else	3
implement	— provide the power and authority necessary to accomplish or put something in effect	10

inadequacy	— not adequate; not enough	10
incentive	— thing that urges a person on; motive	3
indeterminate	— not determined; not definite or fixed	2
inherent	— belonging to a person or thing as a permanent and essential quality or attribute	1
inhibited	— held back; hindered or restrained	9
innate	— existing in a person from birth; natural	2
innovation	— change made in the established way of doing things	9
inquisitive	— asking many questions; curious	5
instantaneous	— coming or done in an instant	2
integration	— act or process or making whole or complete	2
intensifies	— make or become intense or more intense; strengthen; increase	6
interdependent	— dependent upon each other	3
internalization	— relating to the inner being; belonging to or existing in the mind	6
intimacy	— very familiar; very well known; personal	5
intimidating	— making afraid; frightening	6
intricate	— with many twists and turns; puzzling	5

intriguing	— exciting the curiosity and interest	5
latent	— present but not active; hidden	1
mimic	— copy closely; imitate	3
misconception	— a mistaken idea or notion	10
monogamous	— practice or condition of being married to only one person at a time	8
motives	— thoughts or feelings that make one act	2
mutuality	— having done, said, felt by each toward the other	6
necessitates	— to make necessary; require; demand	4
nonverbal punctuation	— same as visual punctuation; it is emphasis in a message which is communicated without the use of words	9
nurture	— bring up; care for; rear; train	1
nutritious	— valuable as food; nourishing	1
optimum	— the best or most favorable point, degree, amount, etc. for the purpose	9
orientation	— bring into the right relationship with surroundings; adjust to a new situation, condition or affairs, etc.	2

paradoxically	— a statement or condition that may be true but seems to say two opposite things	1
passive	— being acted on without itself acting	7
perceptibly	— that can be perceived	5
permeates	— spread through the whole of	4
perpetuate	— make perpetual; keep from being forgotten	4
perspective	— view of things or facts in which they are in the right relations	7
polygamous	— practice or condition of being married to more than one person at the same time	8
potential	— possible as opposed to actual; capable of coming into being or action	1
predestined	— determined or settled beforehand	2
probing	— searching into; examining thoroughly	7
projects	— plan, contrive, or devise; make a forecast for something on the basis of past performance	6
prolonged	— extended in time or space	1
propositions	— what is offered to be considered; proposal	1
prospective	— that is looked forward to as likely or promised	10

relevant	— bearing upon or connected with the matter in hand; to the point	4
reservoir	— a place where anything is collected and stored	1
responsive	— making answer; easily moved	2
retention	— ability to remember; retain	4
revelatory process	— the process of learning received from the Holy Spirit by means of revelation and illumination	3
seclusion	— being kept apart from company; shut off from others	9
senility	— old age; the mental and physical deterioration often characteristic of old age	5
social identity	— the identity of an individual within a social group	8
socialization	— make social; make fit for living with others	6
stature	— height; physical, mental or moral growth	1
survive	— live longer than; remain alive after	1
symbolism	— use of symbols; representation of an idea, quality, condition, or abstraction	5
sympathetic	— having or showing kind feelings toward others	3

technique — a special method or system used to accomplish something — 3

temporal — lasting for a time only — 5

transformation — changing in form or appearance — 2

transition — a change or passing from one condition place, thing, activity, topic, etc. — 1

tyrant — person who uses his power cruelly or unjustly — 8

ultimate — coming at the end; last possible; final — 2

unique — having no like or equal — 3

valid — supported by facts or authority; true — 7

values — something of high worth, excellence, usefulness, or importance — 2

verbatim — word for word; in exactly the same words — 4

visual gestures — movements of the body which visually portray the meaning of a message being communicated — 9

visual punctuation — visual gestures a communicator uses to convey a message — 9

visually — of, having to do with, or used in sight or vision — 10

vitality — vital force; power to live — 1

vocabularies — stock of words used by a person   3

vocations — occupations, businesses, professions, or   10
trades

volitional — having to do with the act of decision or   10
choice

voluntary — done, made, given, etc. of one's free will   6

warrant — a good and sufficient reason   7

Answers to Self-Tests

Lesson 1

1 d) It is subject to growth.

2 e) response to the things noted in answers a), b), and c).

3 b) growth and development which lead toward maturity.

4 c) Spiritual development is needed to prevent spiritual boredom.

5 a) tends to be frail in its infancy.

6 d) can survive spiritually.

7 c) Scripture gives us the diet.

8 b) through constant use of his spiritual faculties has learned to distinguish good from evil.

9 d) cannot receive or understand spiritual truth.

10 a) He exists on a weak, spiritual diet.

11 c) commitment to the Lord.

12 b) the ability to receive and understand spiritual truth.

13 d) response to the Word of God.

14 a) fill the role of active support one needs.

15 b) the application of his knowledge.

Lesson 2

1 b) progressive development of Christlikeness in each believer.

2 a) his original likeness to God.

3 c) Spiritual maturity means to attain to the full measure of Christlikeness.

4 d) grow spiritually.

5 c) develop the full potential of each person for God's glory.

6 a) become Christlike.

7 d) there are stages of development and levels of maturity.

8 c) Realization of spiritual potential and development of whole self-concept.

9 b) nurture spiritual growth.

10 d) en route enablement that helps one move from infancy.

Lesson 3

1 d) a direct way.

2 b) the disciple learns by conforming.

3 c) Christlikeness.

4 a) equipped for service.

5 c) the church is an organism of interdependent parts.

6 a) a broad range of believers exercising various gifts.

7 b) He moves us, often against our will, to conform to the likeness of Christ.

8 c) the use of traditional educational methods.

9 d) personal associations and relationships.

10 b) effective Christian nurture will include both patterns.

Lesson 4

1 b) lessons which require an action response are retained much longer.

2 d) takes advantage of an opportunity to share Christ.

3 b) change for the good is made in one's life.

4 a) Rote memory.

5 c) The lesson content is the key element.

6 e) the things mentioned in a) and b) are correct.

7 b) people hold tightly to their values.

8 c) various levels of learning.

9 a) memorize facts and recall or recognize them at a later time.

10 b) Application.

11 d) Restatement.

12 a) Comprehension.

13 c) most effectively through their seeing and hearing senses.

14 d) the learner hears and then acts upon what he has heard.

15 d) The learner performs best and learns most rapidly when he learns on his own.

16 a) Transfer learning.
c) Recognition.
Rolf is probably using as effective an approach as one could employ with a large class. He shows sensitivity to the learning process by using visuals to reinforce his lectures. Learners are using two senses in his class; however, the response called for is low, since students do not interact with the material. He could enhance his teaching greatly by calling for student interaction with the lessons, asking for application of lessons to daily life, and inviting them to integrate new content with their previous knowledge, permitting it to effect the necessary changes in their lives.

17 b) Discovery learning.
f) Application.
Sheri's approach leaves little opportunity for negative criticism. She is involving students in the learning process so that they learn by both hearing and doing. Their learning is practical rather than theoretical, relating both to their previous base of knowledge and to life situations. Moreover, learning to use the appropriate tools for Bible study is a very positive incentive for students who are motivated to study further on their own. Sheri must be sure to vary the format often enough to avoid getting into a rut.

18 c) helping people to learn.

19 d) discovering information and making desired responses to it.

20 a) using truth as a base for making life choices and guiding actions.

Lesson 5

1 a 5) Middle adolescence.
  b 2) Middle childhood.
  c 6) Later adolescence.
  d 7) Early adulthood.
  e 9) Later adulthood.
  f 1) Early childhood.
  g 4) Early adolescence.
  h 8) Middle adulthood.
  i 3) Later childhood.

2 nonphysical.

3 whole.

4 spiritual, Christ-life, temporal.

5 automatic, nurtured.

6 Imbalance.

7 Personality.

8 heredity, abilities, Intelligence.

9 Environment, culture, values, conduct.

10 will, choices.

Lesson 6

1 d) Biblical facts have all been presented through the impersonal means of recorded revelation.

2 b) they are what God has communicated to us as truth.

3 a) formal and informal patterns.

4 d) appropriate values, attitudes, motives, and behaviors of the Christ-life are absorbed.

5 c) While socialization is useful in learning one's customs, it is not appropriate for nurturing spiritual growth.

6 e) develops a modeling relationship.

7 c) The model must control the relationship.

8 d) have the opportunity to apply what they have learned.

9 b) interaction, intimacy, identification, and imitating.

10 c) significant friends, family members, teachers, and in essence, all Christians.

Lesson 7

1 False.

2 False.

3 True.

4 True.

5 True.

6 False.

7 True.

8 True.

9 False.

10 True.

11 True.

12 False.

13 True.

14 True.

15 False.

Lesson 8

1 False.

2 False.

3 True.

4 True.

5 True.

6 True.

7 False.

8 True.

9 False.

10 False.

Lesson 9

1 d) Sharing groups are the primary element.

2 c) share the life of Jesus with other members.

3 a) significant people who learn to know, love, and accept us for Christ's sake.

4 b) interaction provided by other Christians.

5 c) because of mutuality, self-hood, and relationship.

6 b) the nature of the sharing group enables individuals.

7 a) the group can only meet individual needs.

8 c) involves what is said, how it is said, and the impact it has.

9 a) degree of acceptance members have for one another.

10 d) The kind of social entertainment and recreational activities.

Lesson 10

1 True.

2 False.

3 True.

4 True

5 False.

6 True.

7 True.

8 False.

9 True.

10 False.